TV PROGRAMMING PERSPECTIVES

2nd revised edition

Stephen Winzenburg

TV PROGRAMMING PERSPECTIVES

2nd revised edition

Copyright 2013 by Stephen Winzenburg.

All Rights Reserved.

Published by Media Memories Publishing, Des Moines.

No part of this publication may be reproduced, stored or transmitted by electronic, digital, recorded or photocopied means without the prior written permission of the author.

This is a book of critical commentary and reviews of television programs. All photographs are used for publicity purposes in the context of the reviews and all images are the property of their copyright owners.

This is a revised classroom version of the second edition of the book, abridged with fewer chapters and about one-third fewer pages of text. Special thanks to Lenny Tvedten from the Martin County Historical Society and Sharon Diekman for information on Fairmont, Minnesota's cable system.

ISBN 978-0-9740452-6-9

Library of Congress Control Number for complete 2nd Edition: 2010933837

TV PROGRAMMING PERSPECTIVES

CONTENTS

INTRODUCTION	
Isn't TV Great?	7
CHAPTER ONE	
TV Programming Philosophy	19
CHAPTER TWO	
Cable	37
CHAPTER THREE	
TV Ratings	49
CHAPTER FOUR	
What Makes a Hit?	69
CHAPTER FIVE	
Censorship	93
CHAPTER SIX	
Children & Family Viewing	107
CHAPTER SEVEN	
Television's Greatest Programs	125
INDEX OF SELECTED TOPICS	153

Other books by Stephen Winzenburg

TV's Greatest Talk Shows

TV's Greatest Sitcoms

Watching TV Talk Shows

A Guide to Watching TV Preachers

The Communication Job Search Handbook

Jim and Tammy (with Joe Barnhart)

Introduction

ISN'T TV GREAT?

Television programming has been around for over 65 years and there's no disputing the fact that it has had a major impact on American society. From a two-year-old learning his first Spanish words by watching Sesame Street to the nursing home resident who tries to solve a Wheel of Fortune phrase each night, TV impacts virtually every person from the time they are born (in a delivery "suite" with a TV set) to the time they die (memorialized at a funeral home with a video tribute).

Those who were raised in a time or place where there was little or no television understand that this electronic box has had a large impact on our culture. But if you ask many young adults who grew up with it in their bedrooms, daycares and cars, they would say TV has had little impact on them personally—it's just something that they watch for escapism and they could "live without it" if they had to.

The truth is much more complicated than that. Attempt to wean people from the tube (as I have in my classes) and they quickly discover that they are addicted to the point that they can't go for more than a few hours without turning it on. Like nicotine or alcohol, their bodies and minds are trained to want more and more in order to relive the highs they get during the shows they enjoy watching.

This isn't just an academic theory—it is something proven in the studies conducted annually with students in my TV in

Society class. They are challenged to go on a "TV diet," where they have to gradually work themselves off television and go three days without watching. Their reactions prove that the tube is an alluring drug.

Kevin wrote:

"This diet was probably the toughest thing I have ever attempted... I'm fairly certain I have been emotionally scarred for life... Trying to get me to stop watching TV by putting me on a week-long diet is like treating cancer with a Band-Aid."

"I found it impossible to not watch a few minutes of TV. It would be impossible unless you lived in a remote area. I think we are all naturally led to watch TV and there is nothing we can do about it."

Kevin believes it is part of our physical nature to watch television—which should come as a surprise to anyone born before TV began in the 1940s! The mindset of today's young adult is that watching television is as "natural" as eating or sleeping.

Most people don't want to acknowledge that it's a bad habit or an addiction because that would mean admitting that they have wasted much of their lives. The typical person now spends over one-fourth of their waking hours watching TV and in the average home the set is on for over eight hours a day. To somehow acknowledge that this has any type of negative impact would require viewers to admit they have wasted over one-fourth of their lives.

These TV lovers certainly want to trumpet the positives of the medium—they will share how they had a health check after seeing a morning talk show host bravely have an exam on the air or how their lives changed after reading a book that Oprah recommended or how they grew interested in animal rescue after watching a special on the Discovery Channel. There's no question that TV does lead viewers to do good.

But that's because TV's purpose is to influence viewers to action. Or to be more accurate—businesses believe those who watch television react to what they see. The 2011 Nielsen "Advertising and Audiences Report" estimates that $72 billion was spent on all types of TV ads, based on the belief that consumers will change behavior after watching a commercial for a product.

Viewers respond to advertisements by purchasing what they see on the screen or calling a phone number or checking out a

Website. The $3.8 million 30-second ads in the Super Bowl are proof that even a single message can produce instantaneous results (like 2009's free breakfast ad from Denny's that swamped the restaurant chain with two million customers the Tuesday morning after the big game). That is why over $300 million was spent on TV ads during the 2008 presidential campaign—candidates know that many voters are influenced by what they see in commercials.

Television's impact reaches beyond ads. Sometimes our reaction to what we see on the news is to do something positive for strangers. When a local TV station reports a family's house fire destroys all their gifts two days before Christmas, strangers reach out to help. If we see on TV that a neighborhood is overrun with flooding, we put on our boots and head out to help sandbag.

But despite how TV can lead us to do good or purchase products, more often the reaction is neutral. We just stare at the screen after flipping through the channels and stop at the "least objectionable program" after saying there's nothing on. At times television becomes therapeutic, such as watching an old Boy Meets World episode where all we do is laugh to escape the real world.

So if we all can agree that TV leads us to do good, and TV can relax us by making us laugh, and TV can even cause us to spend our hard-earned money on a product, then why can't we accept the fact that television can also lead to negative reactions?

Some young males respond to violent shows by becoming more physically aggressive. Some young women react to a reality show about bratty girls by copying their attitudes or what they wear. Children, when watching an adult show that parents think is "over their head," hear a word they don't understand and repeat it the next day to other kids at daycare.

We now live in a world filled with psychotics, abusers, addicts, violent co-workers, brats, bullies, students with short attention spans, and just plain nut cases. Could watching that type of behavior on TV for more than four hours a day have anything to do with it?

The hard truth is that you watch television more than you do anything else during your waking hours in your lifetime, and network executives love it because they make a lot of money off you sitting there.

From childhood on, you watch TV more than you spend time eating, bathing, reading, socializing, going to school and even working. **In your lifetime you will spend about 108,000**

hours watching TV. The next closest is about 90,000 hours working—and you only spend about 18,000 in school!

Does your work impact your life? Does going to school affect your life? Do eating, bathing, reading and socializing have any influence on your life? If so, then why don't you think television does the same since you do it more than any of those other things?

Can't those other things have a negative influence as well? If you eat something bad then you spend the night up sick with food poisoning. If you work a lousy job it can lead to anxiety or depression. If you hang around with the wrong friends you can be influenced to drink or do drugs.

If everything else that you do in life has an impact on you, both positive and negative, why would you think that the thing you do most in life would have no negative influence on you? And why does society overlook the powerful impact of the medium?

My conclusion is that it's because we believe that the tube is just an appliance. It is sold in appliance stores. It plugs into the electrical outlet in the wall. We treat it like a refrigerator or a stove or a dishwasher—things that we think only do good for us and have no perceived negatives.

If I said "refrigerators are having a negative impact on society," you would laugh. We accept appliances as necessities that we only use for good and we can't live without them.

Even my student Lori recognized this when she went on her TV diet and wrote,

> *"I guess you could say that I am a TV addict.... I love it too much. Is it wrong to love an appliance?"*

What she and others don't think about is that even neutral appliances can have a negative impact. A leaky gas stove can kill a sleeping family. A faulty dishwasher can spread germs instead of sanitizing. And with one slight turn of a dial, a change in temperature in a fridge can allow bacteria to grow on food that could sicken those who eat it.

If you want to make the television merely an appliance, then you need to accept the fact that appliances can also cause harm if improperly used. What's inside the TV set may be just as tempting to you as that nummy treat inside the refrigerator—but consuming it could harm you if not used properly.

You may scoff at the idea of there being a negative physical impact of watching television, but that is why pediatricians recommend there be limited viewing for children (they recommend one hour a day maximum as the ideal and no TV for children under the age of two). They know that staring at a screen of flashing images harms mental development and leads to other physical problems, which we'll discuss later in the book.

There is no better evidence of this than the story of Dan, my student who struggled with the TV diet. He wrote,

> *"I believe TV ruined my family. No matter what anyone had to say, TV had to come first—a show was on that someone wanted to watch. I started to hate TV, but it was my only way to escape reality."*

> *"My mom became inactive and depressed because she didn't get out of the house much—all she did was watch TV. She gained weight but refused to go see the doctor. She started complaining of severe pains...and eventually went into a seizure and a coma. Four days later her lung had ruptured and she died."*

> *"I blame her death on a few factors: #1—TV.... Now I do not like the company of my current family members, so I use TV as an excuse not to talk to them. So that is probably the main reason why I watch TV all the time."*

Erika wrote about her 16-year-old stepbrother, who had to be held back two years in school and "only smiles when he is watching TV. He has no communication skills and never leaves the house unless it is to go to school." She said that both of her brothers are allowed to watch television all day and "it has driven me out of my parents house. It makes me so angry that they are so lazy. They live and breathe TV." The irony is that Erika has chosen a career in television.

She said her stepbrother is her dad's son who was raised in his younger years by his birth mom and "the TV was his babysitter." He has been to doctors and psychologists, who put him on Prozac. "I wondered what his problem was until I took this class. Although you try to emphasize that TV is not evil, I believe it is. It has taken over my stepbrother's life. The TV is his only friend."

This book, then, is based on the presupposition that television does have an impact on people that watch. It influences individuals, which slowly changes our culture as a whole. Sometimes the impact of TV is positive, very often it's neutral, and there are times it's downright negative.

Other books have avoided the issue while admitting that TV might cause some concerns. In the book *Forbidden Channels*, author Penny Stallings wrote:

> "Does television breed violence? Is it a numbing and addictive drug? Is it destroying the fabric of society or bringing us closer together?
>
> Who knows? Certainly not me. And you won't catch me trying to figure any of it out either.
>
> I'm part of the generation that grew up with the Tube, so for me, television is a given – neither moral nor immoral. I watch it because I love it; and I love it because it's there."
>
> "There is no way for me to separate my television-warped sensibility from what others might consider to be a reality-based view of the world. I am the sum of my total of a lifetime of television-watching and I track my past in terms of particular video benchmarks."
>
> "It comforts me to know that I'm not alone, that it's that way for millions. Because television provides us with a collective reference point."

Note the irony in this addict's admission. She loves the medium and doesn't really care if it hurts people. She says she can't separate TV from the rest of her world. She loves it just because it's there and her life experiences revolve around her television viewing history.

Steven Stark, author of the book *Glued to the Set*, put it this way:

> *"(M)any writers and critics seem to have no problem always treating television as an utter abstraction. 'TV has dumbed down America' they will say or 'Television encourages violence'.*
>
> *Most Americans, however, look at the medium more perceptively. When they think about television they draw on memories of something that's fun and they think about individual shows.... When they talk about the small screen—and they talk about it constantly—they don't discuss the history of broadcast regulation (who would?) but rather their recollection of Lucy on the candy assembly line, O.J. in the Bronco on the highway or Seinfeld and his friends in his apartment.*
>
> *In such a diverse country as the United States, television has supplied everyone with common reference points and a shared culture. Could this be because TV is, in effect, a drug? Maybe. A necessity? That too. But mostly we watch because we choose to and then we watch some more. We love television because of what it has brought us through its vast array of presentations."*

This writer's message is also loud and clear—that we merely love it because it's there and it doesn't make any difference if it causes a drug-like addiction.

In the 1990s, the ABC network decided to run a print ad campaign that screamed the headline, "TV is Great." It was meant to not just promote ABC but to tell people that it was okay to watch television—any television, as much as you want. The ad copy included:

> *"For years the pundits, moralist and self-righteous, self-appointed preservers of our culture, have told us that television is bad. They've stood high on their soapbox and looked condescendingly on our innocuous pleasure. They've sought to wean us from the Boob Tube or the Idiot Box.*

Well, we're here to tell you that television is not the evil destroyer of all that is right in this world. In fact—TV is good. TV binds us together with shared experiences. In the span of ten years TV brought us the downfall of an American president, one giant step for mankind and Charlie's Angels. Can any other medium match TV for its immediacy, its impact, its capacity to entertain?"

Of course a company that makes its profits off viewers watching television is going to claim that all TV is "great" and then ridicule the "self-righteous" that point out the negatives of watching the tube. That's a little like cigarette manufacturers claiming, "Smoking is Great" or distillers saying, "Drinking is Great." Even when those groups advertise they include messages to partake responsibly. Would TV ever do an ad campaign that says "Watch Responsibly?"

Starting in 2008, with the election of Barack Obama being attributed to his use of electronic media, the press went beyond the concept that watching the tube is fun to promoting the idea that television viewing is "intelligent." Writers claimed that shows like Lost, 30 Rock and Mad Men were making this the greatest TV viewing period in history. Even 2012 articles in publications like *TV Guide* have continued to push the idea that comedies like Modern Family and New Girl are "intelligent television."

Entertainment Weekly started the trend with a list of the 25 Smartest People in Television. While a few of them probably are truly intelligent, there were some real head-scratchers. Tyra Banks? Lorne Michaels, producer of Saturday Night Live? Of the thousands of people involved in television, the magazine thinks those represent the "smartest"? Had the writers ever watched their shows?

Tyra had two series that she hosted at the time (a self-titled talk show and America's Next Top Model) and both wallowed in trash. Producer Michaels' Saturday Night Live might have one or two good segments per week but the rest of the program is filled with sophomoric humor and crude language that usually is more stupid than funny.

Another on the smartest TV list was Oprah Winfrey at #6. Winfrey says she does not watch television and doesn't even have a TV set in some of her homes yet she wants to use the medium to "help empower" viewers. If she really believes TV is a waste of time, then why not just tell people to turn off the TV completely like she does?

Seth MacFarlane, creator of Family Guy, topped the TV intelligence list and that is proof that society's standards have changed to the point that childishness and crudeness are considered smart. Anyone who can get away with making $20 million a year for writing and voicing an animated show filled with demeaning potty humor certainly deserves credit for being smart enough to figure out what the FOX network will pay to air.

The problem is that the media equate TV success with smarts but often the two have nothing to do with each other. Less intelligent people catch a break and become successful by being on the right show at the right time (how else do you explain the Kardashians or Snooki and The Situation on Jersey Shore?). Meanwhile many smart, creative people wallow in obscurity or fail to create something that will have mass appeal.

Then there are the millions of viewers who get their "news" from The Daily Show or The Colbert Report. As hilarious as those series can be, their hosts admit that they are spoofing real news programs, not trying to be taken seriously. Yet during every election those comedy programs are shown to have the greatest influence on the young adult vote! What does it say about society's measure of intelligence when Jon Stewart and Stephen Colbert repeatedly scream, "Don't believe any of this," yet viewers trust them more than the serious news anchors?

Why are we as a society accepting Oprah, Modern Family, The Daily Show and Family Guy as the modern definition of smart TV? Is it to make ourselves feel better about mindlessly sitting in front of the tube?

This book is not going to resolve all the answers about whether television is intelligent or entertaining or positive. It is all of those things at various times.

Instead this book is going to attempt to give a unique and at times skeptical perspective on the TV product that we are being sold. Over 300 million Americans consume television programs and 90% pay money to see them on cable and satellite. Even "free" TV costs viewers money because ads are financed by inflated product prices. Let's be intelligent consumers that learn all we can about how television is produced and packaged so that we know what we are buying.

There is nothing self-righteous, judgmental or moralistic about pointing out the dangers of a product on individuals and society. We have warning packs on cigarettes, laws that limit drinking, guidelines for health product claims and government regulations in quality standards for appliance manufacturers.

Let's apply some of those same principles to the appliance that most of us are addicted to—and see what kind of impact TV programming has on society and on individuals.

Introduction Discussion Questions

1. What age range does television reach?
2. Why do people not want to admit to a TV addiction?
3. What is TV's purpose?
4. What's an example of how watching TV can be positive?
5. If TV does lead to good and does lead to influencing purchases, why do networks deny the logic that it must also have some negative influence?
6. Statistically how do the number of hours watching TV compare with other things in our lifetime?
7. Explain how TV is an appliance and how that doesn't mean it's all good.
8. What view of the medium do the students quoted have?
9. ABC said, "TV is Great." What do you think about what their ad?
10. What type of people are on the smartest people list? How do the media decide who is smart? How smart is Oprah?
11. The author thinks it's okay to point out dangers of TV—what does he compare that to?

Chapter One

TV PROGRAMMING PHILOSOPHY

This is a book about television programming, a subject which may seem easy to define. But "television" today means different things to different people. It could refer to:

- A local commercial broadcast on an over-the-air station you can pick up for free (like the local news you get on a TV with rabbit ears and no cable/satellite connection).
- A commercial network broadcast you pick up on a local affiliate (a prime time network show like American Idol that you pick up with rabbit ears).
- A non-commercial local or network program (public TV through rabbit ears).
- A secondary digital TV channel that comes from a local station via rabbit ears, such as channel 13.2 that airs all weather or channel 8.2 that airs old TV reruns.
- A commercial or non-commercial station that you pay to see through cable or satellite and may be broadcast on a different channel (FOX17's broadcast signal is aired on channel 6 on local Mediacom Cable).
- A commercial cable network you see because you pay for a package of channels through a local cable operator (CNN or ESPN through cable coming in from the outside).

- A commercial cable network you see because you pay for a package of channels through a national satellite operator (CNN or EPSN coming from satellite dish on your roof).
- A commercial cable network you see because you pay for a package of channels that are delivered by a telephone operator (CNN or EPSN coming from a home phone service provider like Fios from Verizon).
- A pay network that you spend extra on, above the normal cable or satellite prices (HBO from cable or dish or phone service).
- Special channels you can only access when staying at hotels (Disney World resorts have special tourist channels).
- An Internet download of a broadcast or cable program, either for free or pay, that you can watch on your computer (Hulu, iTunes, NetFlix).
- A DVD or tape version of a show that you pay for or check out from a rental store or the local library.
- A DVR recording of a show on a device like TiVo, which stores programs you select to record but may include downloaded ads you didn't ask for.
- Digital shows you can only pick up with your computer, smart phone or iPad (original content on YouTube and similar sites, not previously seen on broadcast or cable).
- In-store programs that appear on monitors while you shop (with volume up while you shop at Walmart or Hy-Vee).
- Out-of-home viewing in airplanes, at gas pumps or at restaurants.

Those all could legitimately be called "television." But depending upon your age and your viewing experience, your definition may be different from another person's definition.

Picture this intentionally satirical conversation between you and your grandma:

YOU: "What did you do last night Grandma?"

GRANNY: "Oh, I just watched a little TV. I like The Office on NBC."

YOU: "I thought NBC had a football game on it last night?"

GRANNY: "It did—I watched an Office rerun from 2007."

YOU: "Oh, I have the DVD set."

GRANNY: "Well sometimes I catch the reruns on cable or when we're at your parent's house we can see it on satellite. And at the cabin a local station carries the reruns every weeknight."

YOU: "But yesterday was Sunday. It's not on then."

GRANNY: "Oh, I can check out old clips on Hulu."

YOU: "Cool. But I thought you were out walking with Grandpa last night."

GRANNY: "I just watched it on my Blackberry while we were on the path."

So when Grandma said she just "watched a little TV," you could take that literally. She used a cell phone to view a 2-inch version of a rerun on Hulu. To her that was "television," even though she wasn't at home, wasn't watching it being broadcast live over the airwaves, wasn't watching an actual TV station and wasn't even sitting down!

Writer Jim Louderback questioned in *Advertising Age*, "What the heck is a television set?" He said that his 52-inch LCD screen gets programming from DirecTV satellite, his Xbox 360, Netflix on Wii, and YouTube on his Blue-Ray DVD player. He also has a 19-inch kitchen TV that's connected to Boxee, which allows him to download programs from Amazon.com. A 32-inch living room television has a DVR, which automatically downloads movies on demand. His 42-inch plasma screen in his downstairs office has satellite and gets games and videos from Playstation 3. He even has an old computer in the garage that he can hook up to satellite or download videos online.

Virtually none of these "TV sets" get a signal the old-fashioned way, through rabbit ears. The only set he has with a normal TV tuner is analog and gets no regular broadcast channels since the FCC forced stations to go digital in 2009.

In all he counted ten "sets" for a family of three, but none of them actually get over-the-air TV stations and he has to pay for every device to get access to the shows he watches.

How things have changed from just a few years ago! When I was growing up in the 1950s in the southern Minnesota community of Fairmont, I had one free CBS channel that came from 45 miles away in Mankato (which you may recognize as the "big town" they would go visit in Little House on the Prairie). The ABC and NBC affiliates were too distant to pick up a decent signal regularly, though when the weather was right we could get a scratchy image. We had one black and white TV set. If we wanted to watch something, it was whatever CBS had on the air. So I can tell you about the Sunday night lineup of Ed Sullivan Show and the game show What's My Line. I can't tell you anything about any 1950s or early 1960s shows on NBC or ABC based on the original airings of the programs.

Television to me meant the one show I could get from CBS.

Though cable had been available in Fairmont since 1957 (making it one of first 5% of the towns in the country to get cable), the cable system only carried three channels. According to cable company worker Sharon Diekman, in an article found by Lenny Tvedten at the Martin County Historical Society, "Reception was not the best. Every time an airplane went overhead the picture faded."

Not surprisingly, most people did not pay the $5 a month to get three faded channels. Why pay for something that others in America get for free? Those who paid were considered foolish and cable was only available in rural areas.

That changed in 1965, when a new owner came to Fairmont and upgraded the electronics, increasing the system capacity to 12 channels (even though most of those didn't have anything on them at first). The cable system eventually brought in distant network affiliates from over 100 miles away, which meant news from Minneapolis. That started to make it worth the $5 a month and our family signed up. Suddenly we were able to see NBC (The Monkees!) and ABC (Batman!).

    My television definition expanded from one station to include other networks and shows from the Twin Cities. Then when public television started in the late 1960s, we were able to see Mr. Rogers and Sesame Street, which we wouldn't have had without cable.

    After a court ruling allowed cable to expand with new original channels in the late 1970s, what I called television changed again. Suddenly I was able to get a station from Atlanta called WTBS, a news network (CNN), a channel of all sports (ESPN), and a kids network that played old '50s sitcom reruns at night (Nickelodeon).

    Television grew in the 1980s to mean up to 30 channels from around the country. Fairmont cable subscribers could totally ignore local news or Minneapolis teams and instead focus on national events 24 hours a day or watch the previously unseen Atlanta Braves. The irony was that our small southern Minnesota town got many of these channels before major cities like New York because until then many metropolitan areas didn't have cable. No longer were those who paid for television considered foolish!

    Eventually cable expanded with fiber optic wiring that allowed it to add even more channels. Much of this expansion came in response to the start of satellite television service in 1994 and today Dish or DirecTV subscribers can pay to receive up to 700 channels. For about 90% of the country, cable and satellite have became "television."

Today my parents can get about 200 channels on the cable system in Fairmont. Without cable they can still only get two—that same Mankato station and it's HD side channel!

What we call "watching television" has expanded to include online viewing, where you can catch thousands of clips without ever actually sitting in front of a TV screen. People who don't even own a television set can discuss the latest TV pop culture moment from The Daily Show or Saturday Night Live by watching highlights on their smart phones or laptops.

The incredible expansion of television to new technology has resulted in traditional viewership levels of shows dropping as people shift to watching online or playing back DVR-recorded shows. Meanwhile, overall total viewing of all television has continued to increase to the highest level in history. So while the ratings may show that not as many people are viewing a show in a specific time slot, people are watching more television than ever through all formats.

It may not be long before the network prime time structure, centered around programming for the four major broadcast networks, no longer exists. But for now the central driving force of television programming is still what airs on broadcast networks in prime time.

The prime time period, from 7 to 10 p.m. weeknights and 6 to 10 p.m. on Sundays (all times listed in this book are Central time zone), still brings in the biggest ad dollars and the most buzz. Cable networks have started to pull viewers away from over-the-air broadcast networks in prime time, but for now FOX, CBS, ABC and NBC are still leading the way in original programming and income.

When a network airs a show, it must worry about putting it in the right time slot to attract an audience. Some good shows die because they are placed in the wrong time slot. Seinfeld originally was on Wednesday night at 8 and almost no one watched. When Cheers went off the air, NBC switched Seinfeld to Thursday at 8 and it immediately became the #3 show in the nation.

Others thrive as soon as they go on the air, such as The Mentalist becoming a top ten hit in 2008-2009 from the time it started on Tuesday nights following NCIS. It continued to succeed when moved to Thursday nights, where it ranked #7 in 2010 and still was #12 in 2012.

There's usually no way to predict what show will work in what time slot, but many people are paid big bucks to put together a schedule that will attract the largest audience for advertisers.

Programmers start with the philosophy that people watch certain **appointment shows** and then schedule viewing habits around those appointments. In 2012, appointment shows included Sunday Night Football, American Idol, Dancing with the Stars, NCIS and Big Bang Theory. People intentionally tune in or TiVo those shows and often won't miss an episode.

To be a true appointment show you have to be a fairly big hit, ranking in the top 25. Cult favorites like The Office may be appointment shows for the die-hard fans, but the reality is that the show's ratings are so low that it can't really be called appointment television (it has never ranked higher than 52nd in season averages).

Other series may be appointment shows for a short time but then lose steam, either because viewers tire quickly or the network moves the show to a different time slot. The FOX medical series House ranked in the top ten for a couple years when it aired on the same night as American Idol, but when moved to air on its own it dropped to number 42.

The NBC science fiction series Heroes is a recent example of a program that appeared to be one that people would schedule their lives around. During its first season (2006-2007) it peaked with 16 million viewers and was nominated for the best drama Emmy Award. But after stumbling with the second-season storyline the ratings dropped to the point that only fanatics watched. It left the air after four seasons in 77th place and the final episode had only 4 million watching.

A few appointment shows can stay on the air without big ratings. The FOX network keeps Family Guy and The Simpsons on only because they draw young affluent viewers to the network. The animated comedies ranked 70th and 75th overall in 2012 but higher in young adult numbers. America's Next Top Model has stayed on the air for ten years (18 seasons or cycles) even though in 2012 it came in at #172 out of 195 shows.

The prime time schedule is traditionally built around the one big appointment show that people will tune in to watch. Typically this is the 8 p.m. program and it becomes what's called the **tentpole**. As people finish dinner and turn on the TV, viewing levels increase during the 8:00 to 9:00 hour, then viewing levels decline as people start to head off to bed. (The average total viewership is 110 million at 7:00, 118 million at 8:00 and 108 million at 9:00 before dropping to 69 million at 10:30.) The 8 p.m. tentpole show then props up the entire schedule.

The estimate is that about 1/3 of all prime time shows are actual appointment series. The rest are things people watch because nothing else is on, known as "least objectionable programs" (or **the L.O.P. theory**). Networks try to schedule L.O.P. shows that mesh well with the hits, so a success like Modern Family has less popular programs around it that won't make viewers want to turn away. As former NBC programmer Warren Littlefield wrote about L.O.P. shows in his book *Top of the Rock*, "The object was to piss off as few viewers as possible."

The most successful L.O.P. series are often placed right after appointment shows, thriving only because they follow hits. The Julia Louis-Dreyfus comedy The New Adventures of Old Christine was called a hit (even though it had mediocre ratings) after it was placed on Monday night after Two and a Half Men. Once the series was moved to Wednesday almost half the audience stopped watching (the series started with 12.5 million viewers on Monday and by the time it was cancelled in 2010 it was averaging 6.7 million people on Wednesday nights).

Most L.O.P. shows are watched because people want to escape from life and are willing to settle for anything because "there is nothing on." Head PBS researcher David LeRoy said, "People are more interested in the act of watching TV than in watching specific programs." He pointed out that a typical viewer comes to the TV set to be entertained by whatever is on and rarely looks for a specific show.

Note that this is a very different philosophy from how you watch shows online, where you initiate viewing specific programs that you like on Hulu or Netflix. Young adults are now taking more control of their viewing habits and ignoring L.O.P shows in favor of things they like online or recorded on their DVR.

A few L.O.P. shows can actually have longer runs than appointment shows. The typical big hit lasts six to eight years on the air, spending four or five years at the top of the ratings. Programs that are not objectionable can stick around for a decade or more. The Jeffersons, M*A*S*H, Coach, King of the Hill, Full House and Boy Meets World all had their fans and were easy to turn to if nothing else was on—but their mercurial ratings kept them from being true appointment shows even though they lasted longer than many bigger hits.

Sometimes L.O.P. shows, if properly handled, can turn into appointment shows. Two and a Half Men survived for years by airing just after Everybody Loves Raymond. When Ray Romano decided to stop making his Monday night series, CBS moved Two and a Half Men up a half hour into the old Raymond time slot and turned it into a hit that people now tune in for.

One of the best examples occurred in 1991 when Home Improvement premiered as a 7:30 Tuesday night L.O.P. comedy that was to benefit from airing between top-ten shows Full House and Roseanne. The Tim Allen comedy became more popular than those other shows and ABC moved it to a Wednesday night at 8:00 tentpole slot where it became the number one series on television.

Similarly, Big Bang Theory was an L.O.P. show that followed Monday night hit Two and a Half Men but it soon became so popular that CBS moved it to Thursday nights where it became the highest-rated comedy on TV. Ironically in 2012 the network moved Two and a Half Men to the slot following Big Bang on Thursdays, a rare case where the network's programming philosophy flips between two series.

The network wants to keep viewers from turning the channel. It wants to create a strong **audience flow**. That's when people don't reach for the remote after a show ends, looking for something else to watch.

A good example of audience flow would be the 2005 Sunday ABC block where Desperate Housewives at 8:00 led into Grey's Anatomy at 9:00. The ratings averaged 21.7 million for Housewives and 21.3 million for Grey's, meaning almost no one tuned out in between the two shows. The hospital drama became so successful that ABC moved it to Thursday night at 8:00 where it became an appointment show on its own.

Cable networks have begun to find similar success with their own appointment shows. An entire cable network can thrive around one hot series. Project Runway, Hannah Montana, Monk and The Closer became hits, then drew viewers to other shows on their cable networks. The cable advantage is that these original series can run an episode multiple times throughout the week, compared to the major broadcast networks that usually only air a program once a week. For example, a new episode of E!'s The Soup runs twelve times in one week.

A cable network's success can be tied to one appointment show. ESPN has built SportsCenter into an around-the-clock franchise. Bravo found a hit in the Real Housewives of Orange County and cloned it into five other versions. FOX News became the number one information network based on the success of The O'Reilly Factor. And The History Channel went from a sleepy documentary network that no one watched to one of the highest-rated on cable with Pawn Stars, which became the number one series on cable and led to other hot reality shows like Swamp People and American Pickers.

Cable and broadcast networks are now battling to find the next appointment shows. They encourage the creative Hollywood community to come up with ideas that could break a network out from the rest of the pack, like Hot in Cleveland, Bayou Billionaires, Bad Girls Club, The Client List, Swamp People, Celebrity Rehab and Jersey Shore.

The programming process starts with **the pitch**, where producers bring their ideas to a network and make a 15-minute presentation in front of executives. A pitch can range from a dramatic storyline to wacky comedy routine, hoping to attract interest from network bigwigs by presenting the idea in a unique way.

Thousands of pitches occur in Hollywood each year. Some are legendary for their failure. The man who created Last Comic Standing pitched a reality series called Pimp House, where six real prostitutes shack up. The guy who did Fear Factor tried to sell Bangladesh Roulette, where a stadium full of people compete to be picked as the one to have the privilege of putting a gun to his or her head.

The British man who came up with the idea that eventually was called Survivor was such a failure at pitching that he returned to England without a sale after standing in front of all the major networks. Only years later did salesman Mark Burnett take the guy's concept back to the networks and sold it to CBS by including the idea of having sponsors pay to have products placed as rewards for challenges.

The creator of CSI was a tourist tram driver in Las Vegas who did months of police research but could hardly speak when stumbling through his original pitch meeting at ABC, which obviously passed on taking the show. CBS eventually took the series from the high-energy writer but he later found less success pitching the network on a hip-hop reality program.

Full House was pitched as a racy adult comedy called "House of Comics" about three wild single stand-up comedians that live together. The program wasn't sold until it was turned into a family comedy about a softhearted widower with three little girls and his two buddies.

ER's idea was twenty years old and had originally been created as a feature film called "EW." When it's writer Michael Crichton became famous for Jurassic Park, his old hospital drama script was dug up and NBC shot a two-hour pilot called "24 Hours"—which was later renamed ER.

Compared to those that take years to get on the air, other pitches take only moments to sell. Flavor of Love was bought after only 35 seconds with the pitch, "Flavor Flav in a version of The Bachelor." America's Funniest Home Videos was sold in four minutes.

Some pitches come with stars attached or a famous producer. Movie stars Eddie Murphy, Chris Rock, Ben Affleck and Matt Damon have production companies that sold series because the actors came to the pitch meeting. Ashton Kutcher was in on the pitches for ideas he produced like Punk'd and Beauty and the Geek. The same with Conan O'Brien, Jimmy Fallon, Sarah Jessica Parker and Shaquille O'Neal. What network wouldn't want to listen to a pitch from these stars-turned-producers?

Those who create the show and deliver the pitch may not be the ones who eventually bring the show to the air. Tom Fantana, who produced Oz and Homicide, pitched The Philanthropist to NBC as the story of a businessman who wants to save the world after his son's death. The network bought the idea, then turned it into what Fantana called, "some kind of A-Team, Fantasy Island thing." When the creator objected, he was fired from the show he created and replaced by a guy who had done Battlestar Galactica and Bionic Woman.

If the pitch is bought by the network, the next step is to order a **pilot script**. A writer is paid to come up with the first episode of the series. Often the writer is the original creator of the show's concept and after a few months the final script is reviewed by network executives, who may completely change the original plot and characters.

If they like what they read, the networks order a **pilot episode** to be shot. Few pitches ever turn into pilots—only 3 to 5% of the pitch ideas ever get to the pilot stage.

This is the most expensive aspect of creating a series because drama pilots cost up to $4 million to make (though the two-hour pilot of Lost was the most expensive in TV history at around $12 million) and half-hour comedy pilots cost up to $2 million.

A **showrunner** becomes the main producer of the pilot (often the series creator) that negotiates between the network and the creative team. New sets have to be built, production crew hired, original music created and actors have to sign four- or five-year contracts (Steve Carell of The Office said he was originally signed to a seven-year deal and refused to renew in 2011).

According to a recent *TV Guide* story, the average pay per episode for a director is $40,000 and for a writer $32,000. Then the performer salaries can range from "scale," which is the $140 per day minimum that background actors can earn, to millions for the stars.

Ray Romano holds the record for actor's pay, making $1.8 million an episode for Everybody Loves Raymond and getting a percentage of the profits on top of that. Charlie Sheen earned almost $40 million a year for Two and a Half Men. Jerry Seinfeld got $1 million a week for acting but earned even more than the rest by being a producer who makes a percentage off the show's reruns. And, believe it or not, at one point each major voice actor in the Simpsons cast was making close to $10 million a year—for about 70 days work.

Television's highest-paid non-actor is Simon Cowell, who earns almost $50 million for X Factor and other shows he produces (like America's Got Talent). And to think that the unknown Cowell did the first season of American Idol without a written contract!

In all, the major networks spend over $500 million on developing new shows. After around 20 pilots are made for each major network in the spring, executives screen them to decide which will be the few that are ordered for a series.

To decide which shows to put on the schedule, they test the pilots in front of people selected off the street or through random phone calls. I was part of the pilot test for Frasier, which involved watching the show on a special cable channel and then spending a half hour on the phone answering questions. Those questions included (yes, I took notes):

- How much did you watch? At any point was the show boring?
- Would you rate the character of the dog excellent, good, fair or poor?
- Would you watch the show if it was on at the same time as Cheers (odd since they were both NBC series), Murphy Brown, The Simpsons, Roseanne, Cops, and Full House?
- Rate how much you think a family can watch it? What values does it have that you can relate to? How believable it is?
- Which of these words would you use to describe Frasier (they listed 25): Charming? Cold? Intelligent? Friendly? Corny? Funny? Attractive?
- Rate the title. (Well, the show was about Frasier!)

When in May the announcement is made for which pilots are "picked up" for the new fall season, of the 600 to 1000 pitches made to each major network, only 10 to 12 end up on the air. And of those that do make it—60 to 90% will be cancelled within the first year, which means the TV programming business has one of the highest failure rates of any industry.

To put it in perspective, say that you as a college student must write 12 research papers in order to graduate. But you are told that you must come up with at least 600 ideas for papers that you'll present to the faculty members, then you will write rough drafts of about a hundred of those ideas that they can pick from, and when you turn in the final 12 papers at least ten of them are give F's and you're told to start over. So out of all of that work only one or two ideas are successful. That's what happens every year with people who create television programming.

May is also the time when network programmers announce where on the fall schedule the new shows will be placed. The announcements are made one day after another by each network, in front of advertisers in New York City. The broadcast networks try to sell ad executives on buying commercial time in the new shows, so the stars are paraded onstage in often-elaborate production numbers.

The scheduling of the series is one of the most difficult jobs because a network team has no idea what the other networks are going to do. Imagine the surprise in 1994 when both CBS and NBC announced a new Chicago-based hospital drama at 9 p.m. on Thursday nights! One was Chicago Hope and the other ER. The

NBC series with George Clooney won that battle but it's hard to believe that amongst all the thousands of ideas that were pitched that year, two competitors put the exact same type of show on in the exact same time slot.

That is called **head-to-head** programming—where one network competes against the other by putting on the same type of show. Often certain genres of shows work in certain time slots (such as dramas at 9 p.m.), so the idea is that if a competitor's show can't be beat by something different then the opposing network might as well put on something similar. Examples would be the evening newscasts all airing at the same time on the major networks or late night talk shows all competing head-to-head.

The history of television is littered with head-to-head competitors that hurt each other. One of the most famous (and bone-headed) was when FOX aggressively tried to dethrone the Cosby Show on Thursday nights at 7:00 by moving the Simpsons against it. Both were family-based comedies, though some could argue that they attracted different audiences. What ended up happening was that the ratings for both dropped as the audience had to make a choice. It wasn't long before FOX moved the animated series back to Sunday night while Cosby Show never really fully recovered (it dropped from #1 to #5 in the ratings and slowly lost viewers after that).

Something similar happened in the Spring of 2012 when NBC decided to put its new hit The Voice directly against ABC's Dancing With the Stars. Similar competition reality shows, which were each network's highest-series, were put up against each other resulting in both losing viewers.

In recent years there has been such a glut of reality shows and procedural dramas (where the focus is on the details of solving the crimes more than the crimes themselves) that they often have to go up against each other just due to sheer numbers, such as CSI: New York vs. Criminal Minds or top-rated American Idol against the top ten Dancing with the Stars results show. There have even been nights when all five broadcast networks have aired reality shows in the same time slot.

The opposite of head-to-head competition can also happen. It's called **counterprogramming** when one network goes up against a hit by putting on something completely different. The CBS drama NCIS started off as a low-rated spin-off of JAG, only to see its audience grow after hit reality shows Dancing with the Stars and American Idol moved against it. By 2009, NCIS was a top five show that aired at the same time as #1 hit Idol and by 2012 the drama was beating the reality show in some weekly ratings. The reason? People who don't like reality TV wanted to watch something different.

In the 2010-2011 season, CBS tried to go for a younger audience on Thursday nights by replacing longtime hit Survivor at 7:00 with youthful male-oriented The Big Bang Theory. Thursday is often a battle zone because it's a big advertising night for networks. Movie studios are willing to spend big bucks to push films that are opening on Friday.

The problem was that Big Bang then had to compete head-to-head against NBC's Community and 30 Rock, while counterprogramming American Idol on FOX. It was a dangerous programming move because Big Bang had become a top show on Monday nights right after Two and a Half Men—would the audience follow Big Bang to Thursdays?

The answer was a resounding yes—it worked out so well that Big Bang Theory's ratings eventually went up while the shows against it went down. In this case counterprogramming was a good move.

Networks can also use other programming philosophies, such as **strong lead-in** (a network puts a weaker L.O.P. show right after a hit), the **hammock** (a weak show is put in between two strong shows) and **bridging** (letting a show run longer so viewers stay tuned to the next series, like when Idol would run three minutes late and then go directly into Glee).

There is also **stunting**, where a network uses gimmicks to grab viewers away from the competition, such as 30 Rock's live episode or a night of 3-D episodes. The most successful programming stunt occurred in August of 1999, when ABC decided to premiere the new Who Wants to Be a Millionaire almost every night for two weeks straight, with the ratings climbing each night until it became the number one show on television.

One other philosophy is **block programming**, in which a network tries to keep the audience flow by airing the same types of shows all in a row. Examples include the current Sunday night animated block of shows on FOX, the Must-See TV lineup on NBC in the 1990s and the CBS liberated working-women comedies on Monday nights in the 1980s.

The greatest of all block programming was the old TGIF schedule every Friday night on ABC. The name was first put on the program block in October of 1989, with a lineup that included Full House, Family Matters, Perfect Strangers and Just the Ten of Us. Over the next 11 years, youth-based sitcoms filled Friday nights, including Step by Step, Boy Meets World, Dinosaurs, Hangin' with Mr. Cooper, Two of the Kind and Sabrina.

TGIF built on the Friday night foundation ABC had established in the '70s with The Brady Bunch and Partridge Family, and in the '80s with Webster and Mr. Belvedere. The '90s TGIF shows were safe family programs with large diverse young casts. And the network interspersed the shows with relaxed joking around by cast members that would "host" the night.

The concept was so popular that it even inspired spin-offs. ABC started a Saturday night comedy block called "I Love Saturday Night" (with Who's the Boss and Growing Pains) while CBS stole former TGIF series Family Matters and Step By Step for its own "CBS Block Party." In 2010, ABC similarly designated its Wednesday night comedy block (with Modern Family and The Middle) as "Laugh On."

ABC attempted to revive the TGIF brand in 2003 (without stars hosting between the shows) but that two-year incarnation was doomed to failure because it wasn't kids-oriented. Lifeless, adult-oriented comedies like Hope & Faith and The George Lopez Show were promoted as a return to the family sitcom schedule of the past. Yet the network made a major miscalculation of what made the original TGIF series successful by failing to focus the plots around the children.

The TGIF philosophy has been found recently on cable's Nickelodeon (Spongebob, iCarly, Victorious, Big Time Rush) and the Disney Channel, that over the past few years has had Hannah Montana, the Jonas Brothers, The Wizards of Waverly Place, Sonny with a Chance, Good Luck Charlie and The Suite Life of Zack and Cody. Those titles tell you that the most successful family program blocks have revolved around the children.

Chapter One Discussion Questions

1. What different things could the word "television" mean? How does Jim Louderback's home illustrate that?
2. Based on the author's personal story, how has viewing changed over the decades?
3. Define appointment show, how many occur in prime time, and give a current example.
4. How can a show be a hit but not a true appointment show?
5. What L.O.P. shows have even outlasted appointment shows? What is Home Improvement an example of?
6. What is audience flow?
7. What makes cable networks different in how they air appointment shows?
8. How do you know if a pitch is successful? How many pitches become pilots?
9. What's a showrunner? Who have been the highest-paid prime time stars?
10. Give a current example of head-to-head programming and counter-programming.
11. What's so great about TGIF? Who copied it? Where is TGIF today?

Chapter Two

CABLE

Most of the discussion so far has been based on broadcast network programming. That is because for the first 30 years of the television medium, the three broadcast networks were the only commercial providers of original national programming that was seen in a regular time slot. All cable could do in the early days was offer the broadcast networks to homes that couldn't normally get ABC, CBS or NBC.

Cable, originally called CATV for Community Antenna Television, has been around since at least 1950 but was called "fool's television" because homeowners in rural areas far from big cities would pay to see the same broadcast network TV shows that those living in metropolitan areas could watch for free. There was so little interest in cable that by 1970, when cable was over 20 years old, only 7% of the nation was willing to pay for it.

Remember that little hometown of mine, Fairmont, Minnesota? Those of us who lived there had no idea then that we were on the cutting edge of television technology at the time. We thought we were stuck paying for channels that almost everyone else in America got for free. Instead I ended up being one of the first people in the country to subscribe to this revolutionary device!

By the early 1970s our cable subscription money paid for two stations each of CBS, NBC and ABC, along with early public television and a "weather channel" that was a black and white camera pointed at a thermometer, barometer and clock on a rotating drum. The wheel would slowly spin and allow you to read the time and temperature before it would stop and spin back the other direction.

Things started to change in the 1970s when some cable operators invested in specialized networks, the most famous being HBO. Started by Warner-Amex cable system, HBO was a way of bringing recent theatrical movies into the home before the broadcast networks would air them. Cable subscribers would have to pay extra to see these movies early—and at first it wasn't an overwhelming success because cable was not available in many major cities.

HBO was first offered to big city-dwellers in 1972 as "wireless cable," where they could get HBO with a receiving dish (similar to today's home satellite dish) from a microwave signal sent from a local tower. HBO was picked up by some rural cable systems but didn't become nationally prominent until 1975, when the network began satellite broadcasting. In those early years HBO was only on the air from 3 p.m. to midnight.

Broadcasters got nervous about the new competition, along with the fact that they didn't get any money from cable companies that were making subscribers pay for local stations. So broadcasters pushed the FCC to put restrictive rules on cable that would limit its growth. That included dropping the two versions of each network that customers received when the channels aired the same thing. So when CBS in Mankato was airing the same show as CBS in Minneapolis, we were forced to only get the Mankato station while a sign was posted on the distant station's channel saying that FCC rules required that it be turned off.

HBO took the FCC to court and in the landmark 1977 "Home Box Office Decision," the U.S. Court of Appeals chastised the FCC for passing laws that held cable back. They said that the FCC had favored broadcasters and discouraged cable. The court ruled that the FCC "has in no way justified its position that cable television must be a supplement to, rather than an equal of, broadcast television."

So the FCC began tossing out cable rules and CATV began to flourish. Within three years of the ruling a number of major networks started, such as Superstation WTBS, ESPN, Nickelodeon, MTV, Family Channel (now ABC Family) and CNN. People finally had something worth paying for and by 1980 20% of the homes in America subscribed to cable.

But still the broadcast networks and cultural skeptics thought nothing of it. They scoffed at the idea that the majority of people would ever pay to watch television. *Newsweek* magazine predicted in 1981 that cable would "never reach a majority of homes." It said that at the most only 40% of the people would ever be willing to pay for what they watch.

In 1985 I participated in the International Radio-TV Society's Faculty Fellowship program, where I went to New York City, met with network executives and was part of the TV programming competition (I was part of the group that won). It was there that an NBC vice president stood before us and said that networks were not worried about the competition because viewers would never accept cable the way they do broadcast television.

The irony, of course, is that 25 years later Comcast Cable announced it was purchasing NBC.

By 1990, 60% of homes in America had cable. Then with the advent of satellite services like DirecTV and Dish in 1994, more cable networks started and people subscribed to the point where today about 90% of the homes in America pay to get cable channels either through a cable system or satellite operator.

The broadcast networks are scrambling to figure out how to survive against the competition. They waited too long, thinking the old model of advertiser-supported broadcast television would remain the best way to make profits. The reality is that cable networks can make hundreds of millions in profits without ever having a hit show because they collect fees from subscribers and are not solely dependent upon advertising revenue.

Today cable networks draw about 2/3 of all TV viewing time, win most of the major Emmy Awards and make higher profits than broadcasters. That is why every major broadcaster eventually started or bought cable networks in order to stay alive.

NBC, which used to ridicule cable, now owns CNBC, MSNBC, Bravo, E! and many other cable networks. The head of NBC even told stockbrokers that the NBC broadcast network represented only about 5% of the company's earnings and that cable was the "most important part" of the media company! That's quite a change from the days when the network didn't take cable seriously.

ABC, which is owned by Disney, takes in about one-fourth the amount of money that sister network ESPN makes. ESPN gets over $1.5 billion a year from ad revenue and around $5 billion from subscriber fees, even though ABC has many more viewers.

Whenever a cable network increases subscription prices, the operators can pass the cost along to customers. For many years the cost to operate a cable system was relatively low. Then times got tough in the 1990s with the need to compete with satellites by upgrading cable systems to fiber optic, which cost millions to replace the old co-axial cable in order to expand channel lineups. That is part of why cable bill inflation shot up at a higher rate than just about any other consumer item.

The FCC also bowed to broadcaster demands that cable systems pay to carry local over-the-air signals. Until 1994, local stations didn't get paid for being carried on a cable system. The FCC then pass a two-option rule:

- One is called "must carry," where a local broadcaster can force the cable system to carry its signal for free. This would be used by smaller independent and religious stations that struggle to get carried on cable systems.
- The other is called "retransmission consent," where the cable company wants to carry a popular local broadcaster but must get permission first. Often that consent comes with some form of compensation. This would be for the major local stations that a cable operator needs to carry in order to attract local customers.

Retransmission consent has become the most contentious rule in recent broadcast history because it has pitted two giants, over-the-air broadcasters and cable systems, against each other in a struggle for subscriber money.

For the first few years cable refused to pay broadcasters as part of retransmission consent agreements and instead they would negotiate deals for special channels. So, for example, instead of paying local stations to carry FOX programs, cable systems agreed to carry the new network FX.

But by 2000 the battle came to a head when in the big local ratings month of May, Time Warner cable dumped ABC stations after failing to work out a retransmission deal. It happened on the biggest TV night of the year, with the much-publicized first celebrity edition of Who Wants to Be a Millionaire featuring Rosie O'Donnell. In Time Warner cable markets, the screen went blank, replaced with a message that said the network would not air and it was ABC's fault. Viewers flooded the cable operator with calls. After 36 hours ABC was back on and it made the cable system look bad even though the network deserved part of the blame.

Since then similar contentious negotiations have resulted in channels temporarily dropped from cable systems. The Sinclair Broadcast Group's local stations fought Mediacom and other cable systems, demanding up to 50 cents per subscriber for retransmission consent (an amount higher than many of the big cable networks receive). Mediacom took Sinclair to court without success, then went to the FCC before being turned away. It became a poker game of bluffing—trying to see who will budge first.

The local FOX station in Des Moines, which is owned by Sinclair, got into the scrap and was off the cable system for three weeks at the start of the American Idol season. The loss of just that one channel from the cable lineup caused so much commotion that in Des Moines alone the cable company ended up distributing over $1 million in rabbit ears so that cable subscribers could continue to watch Idol. The FOX affiliate took out newspaper ads offering Mediacom customers $150 to switch to DirecTV, which had an agreement to carry the local station.

The battle in Iowa only ended two days before the Super Bowl because customers in Cedar Rapids and other markets where Sinclair owned CBS affiliates were going to lose access to the big game unless an agreement was reached. Yet the Sinclair FOX station in Spokane was off the cable system for over a year before it came back on!

It happened again in summer of 2007 when the Big Ten Network premiered and wanted $1 per subscriber per month to be carried on cable systems. Mediacom put them on a special sports tier, which meant only those that paid extra could get the channel.

The Big Ten wanted it on the basic tier so everyone would have to pay, claiming every customer in a Big Ten state would want to watch the new channel. But the fact is only about ¼ of the homes watch sports on cable, so ¾'s of the people would be paying for something they don't watch.

At one point Mediacom proposed that the University of Iowa help pay for the costs of putting the channel on basic cable! They wanted tax dollars be used to help a private cable system make a profit.

Other than that bone-headed suggestion, Mediacom had every right to put the sports channel where it wanted. The Big Ten Network isn't a local broadcaster, so the retransmission consent rules don't apply. There are over 400 non-local cable channels out there and Mediacom doesn't "have to" carry any of them. If it does choose to carry a channel it can negotiate what tier that network is placed on.

The Big Ten Network was attempting to bully Mediacom and mistakenly thought there would be a groundswell of support from fans to get it carried on the basic tier. They didn't figure that most customers don't want to see their monthly bills raised just to carry a few Iowa games. Ultimately it went on the special tier before the network changed its high-priced demands.

Expect more temporary local station blackouts on cable. Even though the average local station is getting paid 20 cents per home per month (which adds up to $200,000 a year for a local station in Des Moines), some want it increased to 50 cents a month. When they see cable customers willing to shell out $100 a month for all those channels, local stations and broadcast networks want a bigger part of it.

These are the 2011 numbers for the top 25 cable networks that subscribers pay for. Note that these are not the number of people that watch these networks, but the number of homes that can get the networks via cable, satellite or phone subscriptions:

Rank	Network	Subscribers
1	TBS	102,800,000
2	Discovery	101,900,000
3	USA Network	101,800,000
4	TNT (Turner Network Television)	101,700,000
4	The Weather Channel	101,700,000
6	Nickelodeon	101,600,000
7	Food Network	101,400,000
8	ESPN2	101,000,000
8	C-Span	101,000,000
8	CNN	101,000,000
11	TLC	100,800,000
11	ESPN	100,800,000
11	HGTV	100,800,000
11	Spike TV	100,800,000
11	A&E	100,800,000
16	Lifetime Television	100,700,000
17	MTV	100,600,000
18	History	100,300,000
18	Cartoon	100,300,000
18	Comedy Central	100,300,000
21	Disney Channel	99,900,000
22	VH1	99,800,000
23	ABC Family	99,700,000
23	TV Land	99,700,000
23	CNBC	99,700,000

Source: SNL Kagan. Data from Economics of Basic Cable Networks, 2011

The top networks in terms of subscribers don't necessarily make the most money. Here are the ones that charge the most per home:

Cable Network Retrans Estimates	
ESPN	$4.40
TNT	$1.02
Disney Channel	$0.91
NFL Network	$0.73
FOX News	$0.70
ESPN2	$0.58
USA	$0.57
TBS	$0.50
FX Network	$0.43
MTV	$0.35
Average	$1.02
Average (ex-ESPN)	$0.64

Source: SNL Kagan

Note that while ESPN easily makes the most money of all cable networks (about $5.3 billion a year if you multiply $4.40 a month times 100.8 million subscribers times 12 months), it only comes in 11th on the list of number of homes that receive it. Even ESPN2 is in more homes (probably because it costs so much less)!

On the other hand a major network like TBS, which is in more homes than any other, takes in less than one-eighth ESPN's amount at $616 million. And big networks like The Weather Channel and C-Span get mere pennies a month from each home.

A CABLE NETWORK'S NAME

Flipping through today's ever-expanding cable channel listings has become a game of "guess the network." CURRENT, G4, DIY, WE, LMN. Even though these networks spend millions in branding, viewers are often left confused by names that have little meaning.

The Hub is a meaningless moniker that is actually a new children's channel from Hasbro (it used to be called Discovery Kids). OWN sounds like a shopping channel but is really Oprah Winfrey's network (that used to be called Discovery Health). BBTV may sound like a gun channel, but it's actually family-oriented

"Better Black Television" from rapper Master P. And the vague title of Aspire has been given to a new network owned by Magic Johnson.

Gone are the days when it was easy to remember that CNN meant it was a network that carried news on cable. Today the letters in a channel's title no longer have to stand for anything. And often the more "hip" a network has tried to sound in order to attract young people the less identifiable the brand, such as The N, which is now known as TeenNick, and FUSE, which started as MuchMusic.

The SciFi network was an easy brand to identify and seemed to be a good example of a cable network name that made sense. Yet the owners changed it to SyFy in 2009 and received universal derision for the ridiculous new spelling. The network executives claimed to find the original term "limiting," associated with geek fans of space programs. According to network president David Howe, the change to SyFy "made us feel cooler, much more than cutting-edge, much more hip." Everyone else called it a mistake, especially combined with the network's meaningless tagline "Imagine Greater."

The truth was that the owners were not able to trademark the channel's original name since it's a general description of a genre that has been around for decades. So in order for the network to make money on its name through branding and products, it had to change the lettering.

Many of these changes confuse audiences, such as Court TV switching to TruTV or the Outdoor Life Network becoming Versus which then became NBCSports Network. Spike TV used to be TNN, which originally meant The Nashville Network before it became The National Network. Confused yet?

A&E (Arts & Entertainment) and Bravo started out as identifiers that used to make sense when they aired high-class music and dance. But their programming is now mostly low-class reality and a proper change in the networks' names has not occurred.

Others, like GSN, try to increase branding by shortening what they call themselves. It's no longer the Game Show Network, just as TLC no longer means The Learning Channel and IFC is no longer Independent Film Channel. The networks simply go by their initials.

MTV had always stood for Music Television but twenty years ago started wandering from its original vision to become a network filled with programs. It wasn't until 2009 that the channel officially dropped the name Music Television from its logo and now is just known by its three letters.

VH1 used to play video hits before it also became a reality-based programming network. AMC (originally American Movie Classics) now has movies that aren't all classics and has added traditional scripted shows that aren't movies. The Cartoon Network even has non-animated series with live action.

USA Today had a front-page article that said, "Many cable networks are scrambling to broaden their audiences by reaching beyond their original mission." Like when SyFy added a cooking show, game show and professional wrestling, which have nothing to do with the science fiction theme. But according to the daily newspaper, the channel's president David Howe claims the "perception" that the channel is strictly science fiction "is very narrow." That proves that programmers often don't understand their own brand.

TVLand is one of the best examples of a brand changing from its original vision. The former home of all-classic television first expanded by airing silly reality shows featuring old stars like Mr. T, Farah Fawcett and George Foreman. Then it added reruns modern fluff such as Extreme Makeover: Home Edition. The network now promotes itself as a baby boomer destination by airing the original sitcom Hot in Cleveland and old movies like "Top Gun." TVLand's name no longer means it's just classic television.

Contrast that with ESPN, which has become the model for great cable network branding. Studies show that ESPN achieves higher name recognition than ABC, so the broadcast network calls its game coverage "ESPN on ABC." And the viewers think nothing of a broadcaster promoting a cable network.

I discovered that although everyone knows that ESPN is synonymous with "sports," many of its viewers have no idea what the letters ESPN stand for. I asked the student-athletes in my "Sports and Media" college course and none could explain the abbreviation.

When they were told it originated as the "Entertainment and Sports Programming Network," most of the SportsCenter fanatics still failed to retain the information. The question on the final exam seemed simple: "What do the letters ESPN stand for?" All remembered the word "sports" and most recalled "network." Some of the class even got "entertainment" right. But that little "P" gave these addicted viewers the most trouble.

"Entertainment Sports Publishing Network," wrote Jeremy. Well, the network does have a magazine.

"Entertainment Sports Production Network," answered Troy. Yes, it certainly does that too.

One wrote "E. Sports Public Network," and he may have been studying with baseball player Heath who wrote "Exclusive Sports Public Network."

It probably doesn't matter to the Bristol bigwigs that many of the small-town athletes that watch the network don't know what the letters represent and can't even recall them after being told. After all, these are the same kids that don't have a clue what AT&T or KFC stand for. ESPN's four-letter brand is familiar because it hasn't changed in 30 years and multiple generations have now grown up recognizing it as the premier sports network.

The right identifier can make the difference between failure and success. "FBC" started in the mid-1980s and splashed its shining logo across the press conference it held with its initial star, Joan Rivers. But no one has called it FBC since.

The Fox Broadcasting Network wisely dropped the three-letter abbreviation to simply call itself FOX. And for the past few seasons prime time viewers found the brand name easy enough to remember that it was the number one television network in the young adult demographics. Proof that proper network branding works.

Chapter Two Discussion Questions

1. What's CATV?
2. Why was cable called "fool's television"? What is "wireless cable"?
3. Trace the percentage of homes that had cable over the decades.
4. Explain the Home Box Office Decision.
5. Give evidence of the ways that cable has now surpassed broadcast network TV.
6. How do cable ratings not correspond to which networks make the most income?
7. Explain the two aspects of the 1994 FCC ruling.
8. Explain a recent retransmission battle.
9. What surprises you about the cable networks that are in the most homes?
10. How has cable network branding become confusing?
11. What do student athletes forget about the ESPN name?
12. What is FBC and what does it teach us?

Chapter Three

TV RATINGS

Success or failure of commercial television programming is usually determined by one thing: the Nielsen ratings.

The audience estimates from the A. C. Nielsen Company are the measuring stick used for telling how many people are tuned in to a program. Unlike using a cup measure in baking or a ruler for length, the ratings are not an exact science—they are an approximation of what the company estimates the audience to be.

Nielsen says in 2012 there are 289 million American television viewers in 114.1 million homes with TV sets. While that may seem like a lot, those numbers have dropped the past two years due to a number of young adult households getting rid of the TV and watching shows only online.

The average person watches five hours and seven minutes of television a day—over 153 hours a month, 1840 hours of television a year. Combine that with over 400 channels available to many homes and you see that it is impossible to measure what each individual watches. A cost-effective system is needed to estimate what people are watching without spending the billions it would take to survey every single person about their viewing habits.

Ratings use a scientific method of randomization to attempt to assure that the estimates are the best "educated guess," similar to methods used in opinion polls. About 18,000 homes are equipped with "people meters" that instantly record who is watching what on a TV set. The prime time network viewing information is downloaded overnight and collated by the next morning so that television executives, producers, stars and advertisers can all see how successful they were attracting an audience.

Local People Meters

People meters measure both national viewership and, in major markets, local ratings. To use the people meter, viewers punch in that they are in the room watching by using either a set top box or a remote control. It is a tedious process that requires the person to check in and out every time they enter or exit the room. That leaves a greater chance for error since many people don't punch in or out, so every few minutes a light flashes asking participants to confirm if they are still watching. Namely, it's annoying, which may contribute to inaccuracy by users.

We know that the ratings estimates are not perfect—if American Idol is said to be the number one show for the week with 21 million viewers (as it was for the final episode of 2012), the Nielsen company and the TV industry understand that this is merely a guess based on scientific data. The actual number is probably somewhere between 20 and 22 million with 75% certainty. Does that mean 40 million or 10 million could be watching? Yes, but not very likely. As long as those 18,000 homes with people meters are selected randomly to fairly represent all the homes in the country, then the system is considered scientific even though there is known chance of error.

No matter how scientific the ratings claims to be, Americans remain skeptical of the Nielsen Company. A survey showed that 55% of the country knows what the Nielsen ratings are, but two-thirds of those that know about them don't trust Nielsen.

Those that struggle with the idea of accepting the Nielsen ratings as estimates should compare it to baseball. An umpire calling balls, strikes and outs is not an exact science but an educated guess. Even with an occasional disagreement over a ruling, fans and players must accept the umpire's call even with a chance of error—it's just how the game is played.

The Nielsen Company is the television umpire, making the calls with rules that everyone has agreed to play by. Not everyone is going to be happy with every decision, but, for better or worse, it's the way the TV game is played.

The ump ultimately has a role in deciding which team wins and when a baseball team keeps doing well, more fans fill the stands and the team owners make more money. When the Nielsen Company says that a TV show is winning the ratings race, networks can raise the prices they charge advertisers and make a bigger profit.

From the people meters Nielsen gathers information that is reported in a variety of ways. "Viewers" are the average number of individual people watching a show for at least six minutes. Note that viewer ratings average the number of people watching over the course of the program. When the winner was named on American Idol in 2010, 18.8 million people watched the start of the show but the audience built so that two hours later there were 29.3 million people watching the winner announced. The average was 24.2 million and averages are what get compared in the weekly rankings.

A **household rating** is the percentage of homes watching a show. A **share** is the percentage of homes watching compared to other shows on at the same time.

While there used to be programs that would attract huge percentages of viewers, the fact is that today most ratings and shares are small. In 2012 the top show on television, Sunday Night Football, had a 12.9 rating (less than 13% of the homes watched) and a 20 share (one out of five TV sets turned on watched).

Because advertisers are interested in reaching younger demographics, a rating and share is also reported for each show in the 18 to 49-year-old category. For the 2011-2012 TV season, Modern Family was the #17 show overall in the ratings but with the young adult audience it ranked fifth with a 5.5 rating and 15 share, meaning that five-and-a-half percent of the 18-49 year old households watched the series.

To make it even more confusing, a program can have a higher rating than others but not have the biggest audience because the "rating" and "share" are based on homes, not total viewership. For example, big news was made in Spring 2012 when Good Morning America beat the Today Show in the morning ratings for the first time in 15 years in total viewers. GMA averaged 5.21 million people compared to Today's 5.12 million, but GMA's 3.8 "rating" (percentage of homes watching) was lower than Today's 3.9! So a slightly higher percentage of homes watched Today, but there were more people in those homes watching Good Morning America.

When results are reported each week, the popular media usually fail to note that these are just estimates and that they are not indisputable facts. To claim "Good Morning America beat the Today Show" is not the same as saying, "The Lakers beat the Celtics." With the chance of error figured in, the results between the two morning shows are just too close to state as facts.

Media writers also spin the numbers into whatever story they want, often based on press releases from the networks. A publication like *Entertainment Weekly* is notorious for twisting numbers, so you should not believe everything you read. An online EW story about Family Guy in May of 2012 was titled, "Family Guy rules on night of finales." That's quite a headline for a show that came in 70th place for the season—that's right, 70th.

EW wrote that Family Guy came in first place among 18-49 year olds that night, which was true based on "preliminary estimates." What they ignored in order to get that headline was that those numbers were down 3% from the previous year and that the show actually was beat by its competitors when all viewers were taken into consideration. Celebrity Apprentice and a Tom Selleck Jesse Stone movie easily beat Family Guy in total viewers—so how could EW claim "Family Guy rules"?

The story even reported that Family Guy ended the season as "the most popular show among adults 18-49," which was completely false—it came in 21st in the demographic. Instead the headline should have been "Family Guy ends season down" or "Family Guy beaten by Apprentice."

Meanwhile, the same entertainment writers talked about American Idol being "down" or "losing" (the EW online article was titled "American Idol finale lowest rated ever") when it was the top show for the week and the #2 show for the season both in overall viewership and in the 18-49 demographic.

So they spun low-rated Family Guy as a success and highly-rated Idol as a failure. Don't believe what you read—Idol has many more viewers, and young adult viewers, than Family Guy.

Another aspect that makes analyzing ratings confusing is that since 2007 Nielsen has expanded its national ratings to include DVR viewing and commercial minutes. There are a number of summaries that are released based on ratings data, but the major reports include:

-- **"Live" viewing**. Not "live" in the sense that it's not on film or tape, but "live" meaning people watch the show when it originally airs and aren't watching a recording of the program. About ¾ of all prime time viewing is done live—but young adults only watch 59% live. These numbers are available the morning after a show airs.

-- **"Live plus" recorded viewing.** This takes the original live numbers and adds DVR information in a variety of reports, including "live plus same day" (people who play back the DVR that day), "live plus 1" (includes playing the show back on DVR the next day), "live plus 2" (adds DVR viewing within two days later), "live plus 3" (DVR added up to 3 days later) and "live plus 7" (DVR playback up to a week later). The reason they stop at seven is Nielsen found that almost no playback occurs after one week.

It takes about two weeks to get the 7-day "plus" DVR viewing information processed. So when the original Nielsen numbers are released for the "live" viewing, those numbers could change weeks later when the DVR information is added in.

Some shows gain an additional 20 to 50% from time shifting, usually from young adults. In 2012, Modern Family went from 11.9 million viewers that saw it live to 16.7 million total after 4.8 million DVR viewers were factored in. Other top DVR shows in 2012 were The Mentalist, Hawaii Five-O, NCIS, Criminal Minds and The Big Bang Theory. This trend has led to an unusual cultural crisis. Before tapes and DVR machines, there were "water cooler shows," programs that people would talk about the next day during a break at work. But now if you bring up something you saw last night on TV, people scream at you not to spoil anything because it's on their DVR and they haven't watched it yet!

-- **Commercial ratings called "C3".** This report goes minute-by-minute through the commercial breaks on the "live plus 3" ratings and tells how many people stay tuned for ads.

Believe it or not, there's only a 6% drop-off for commercials during live shows and only 10 to 20% that don't watch ads during recorded shows. Which leads to the question--why would people watch commercials when they have recorded the show and can forward through the ads?

-- Ratings for double airings. If a program is run twice on a cable network, often the results will be combined when reported to the public. So when a new episode of Jersey Shore runs five times during the same week, MTV could claim that "16 million people tuned in" by adding all viewings together. But you can't compare that to just one airing of a competing show.

NBC did this in 2012 when America's Got Talent with Howard Stern premiered and a network ad claimed that something like "32 million people tuned in to watch." To get to that number they would need to have counted the repeat airing of the show that week, along with the people who tuned in for a few minutes and then tuned out. The truth? The show only had 10 million average viewers for its first airing, down 32% from the previous year and was considered a failure.

Nielsen does not report combined airings but only individual showings of a program. So even though it may be technically true that a larger number of people watched if you combine all the different airings of an episode, to play the ratings game fairly the only the original airing should be used for ratings comparison purposes.

The press can choose to report the numbers however they want based on reporters' biases and desire to promote hip, progressive programs. HBO tends to get the biggest benefit from this because the pay cable network will often repeat an episode of an expensive program over and over. So when you read (as EW reported) that Game of Thrones "is averaging a whopping 10.4 million viewers," realize that the HBO show is only getting a 3.7 million average to watch the first airing and the higher number comes from adding together repeat airings on multiple platforms.

-- Cable ratings in the cable universe. Cable ratings have their own peculiarities because they come in two versions. One is when it is reported like the rest of television, based on the 114 million homes that have television sets.

But another way is when these numbers are reported based on the "cable universe." Each cable network has a different number of homes that subscribe to it (as shown in chapter two)—ESPN is in over 100 million homes, while ESPN Classic is in 64 million homes. When Nielsen reports a 5 rating in the cable universe, that rating is based on the percentage of homes that subscribe to the network. A 5 cable rating for ESPN would represent 5 million homes (five percent of 100 million homes) while a 5 cable rating for ESPN Classic would be 3.2 million homes (five percent of 64 million that subscribe).

Namely, in the world of cable all ratings are not the same. So Nielsen reports cable numbers two ways: the rating based only on the total number of homes that get that network (cable universe) and the rating based on all the 114 million homes in America (just like broadcast network ratings).

For example, the 2005 Kirstie Alley series "Fat Actress" premiered with a 4.1 cable rating on Showtime and the network was bragging about the huge audience—except that it was 4.1 percent of the small number of homes that get Showtime. In the national household ratings the program only earned a .62 rating, less than one percent of all homes in America.

There are a number of flaws in the weekly Nielsen ratings. One is that it doesn't include online viewing, so if you watch a show on Hulu the day after it airs on TV the ratings don't include you in the results. Also, household ratings are only taken for those ages two and up, so small children are not counted.

The company does not measure most out-of-home viewing. Viewers not counted in the ratings include those who watch in a hotel, from a hospital bed, at a vacation home or in a bar. That means the numbers you see from Nielsen are even more inaccurate than previously mentioned because they reflect only in-home viewing.

The company finally addressed part of this problem in 2007 when it began measuring college dorm viewing. For over 50 years the millions of young adults who went off to school were never counted in the ratings. That meant programs like Jimmy Kimmel, The Daily Show and Monday Night Football did not have a large part of their audience counted. That has now changed and ratings for sporting events, talk shows and MTV reality shows have all have seen increases due to the inclusion of college viewers.

Most surprising is that in the Internet age the numbers for total television viewing have remained high. Despite predictions of computer usage taking away from the time people spend in front of the tube, audiences in 2011 actually watched more TV than ever before and 2012 numbers only dropped 30 seconds a day from the previous year. So the idea that online video watching has decreased home TV viewing is just not true.

ABC took a closer look at ratings information and found that some programs are much more popular than thought. They used the live-plus-7 results and excluded reality results shows or programs with less than nine episodes. Those types of restrictions skew the results, but what ABC provided was still eye opening.

They figured out which programs had the most people that watched at least once during the season for at least six minutes. These could be people who watched each week or tuned in just one episode for ten minutes. They are listed under "total" below and are compared to the average number of viewers each week.

	TOTAL	AVERAGE
Sunday Night Football	130 million	18.8
60 Minutes	122 million	13.3
American Idol	113 million	24.7
Dancing with the Stars	106 million	19.7
America's Funniest Videos	92 million	7.5
NCIS	91 million	18.7
20/20	88 million	6.5

So while Sunday Night Football averaged only 18.8 million viewers on a normal week in the 2010 season, 130 million people tuned in at any point during the year for even a few minutes. ABC was interested in this analysis because some of their lower-rated programs (like 20/20 that came in 76th in the overall ratings) were actually watched by a large number of viewers who just don't tune in each week or watched for just a few minutes.

The ABC study shows that around half of all viewers watch television alone and those numbers are increasing. About 53% of all TV viewing was done solo, with dramas being the most watched alone and Private Practice on top with 64%. On the other side, America's Funniest Home Videos and American Idol are the programs most watched with others with 53% group viewing.

Overall the survey showed that reality TV does much better than it is given credit for. It is the most consistently watched, attracts extra DVR viewers and has the most multiple-person viewing. And yet fans of Survivor and American Idol only watch one-third of the episodes on average.

NETWORK SPIN

All ratings must be interpreted, filtered, analyzed and put into context. The entertainment press is not doing it, because it's not in their best interest to give you an objective perspective on what's really popular on television. Instead the media are in a competition to attract consumers by hyping stories that draw you to their magazines, newspapers, TV shows or Websites.

So magazines like *TV Guide* and *Entertainment Weekly* do cover stories about shows that have a relatively small number of viewers, such as Community, True Blood and even Downton Abbey. The reason is that the viewers these shows do have are rabid and willing to pay money to buy the magazines.

So to make money, these "journalists" sell out by making a TV show look much more popular than it is. Take the February 2012 Entertainment Weekly featuring three different covers of True Blood (the composite is below but each was a different full cover).

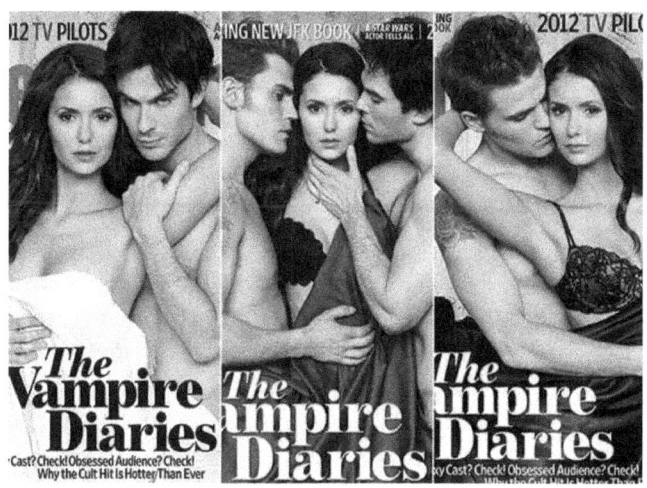

The sexually provocative poses were meant to cause people to pick them up and buy them. But even more disturbing was the line on the cover that said, "Why the Cult Hit is Hotter Than Ever."

Really? A "hit"? Take a look at the show's numbers. Of all the programs on broadcast network prime time in 2012, Vampire Diaries came in 168th place. It averaged 2.78 million viewers and even in the young adult demographic it placed 139th. And as far as it being "hotter than ever"? The ratings were down 7% from the previous year.

So one sentence on the cover alone proves that the "journalists" at Entertainment Weekly are misleading you. But they won in the game of selling issues and impressing fellow media writers, who tore up the Internet to talk about the racy covers. They cared more about buzz and money than truth.

The magazine has done the same with True Blood, Revenge, Parks & Recreation and Gossip Girl. Mad Men has been on the cover multiple times even though less than one percent of the U.S. population watches it.

Meanwhile there is a show that deserves the cover of the pop culture publication—NCIS! It is the highest-rated scripted show on television and unlike almost every other series its ratings have gone up over the past nine seasons (unheard in terms of ratings longevity). It finished the 2012 season with its biggest audience ever, 19.49 million people, and in 3rd place in the overall ratings. Six times as many people watched NCIS as Vampire Diaries, making it truly "the cult hit" that is "hotter than ever."

It was ironic then to read an online article from an EW writer about the program that started out by saying, "NCIS often gets a bad reputation..." Duh! The magazine itself gives it that! While the audience loves the show, media critics ignore it because it's old and repetitive. Instead they go for the edgy, outlandish programs and then try to turn them into successes by claiming they are "hits." (More about that in the next chapter!)

Another example is that in 2012, for the first time in TV history, a sports program was the #1 show of the prime time television season. Sunday Night Football dethroned American Idol's seven-year run as the top show on television. That led some writers to claim that Sunday Night Football was "bigger than ever."

Well...not exactly. The ratings for the program were actually DOWN compared to the previous year! It's just that football numbers were down less than the dramatic drop in Idol viewership. And while the hyperventilating press claimed that football "set records," the truth was that NFL football numbers were down 2.1% and ESPN's games dropped almost 10%! Actual viewership numbers for football were much higher in the 1970s and 1980s.

Some of the blame falls on the networks that attempt to spin numbers to make today's programs sound more successful than past programming. They take "facts," pull them out of context, then issue a press release only to have print and online writers reprint the details no questions asked.

In the most blatant example of a network redefining how numbers are reported in order to skew the truth, NBC claimed that the summer 2008 Olympic games were the "most-watched event in U.S. TV history." And virtually every media outlet repeated that statement unchallenged from NBC's press materials.

The problem is that it was just not true. NBC combined all of the viewers from all of its networks on all of the days of the Olympics, then called the entire 18 days on multiple networks a "single event" in order to make the claim that it was the most-watched event in U.S. TV history.

Any major TV corporation could take all of its networks, combine their viewership over an 18 day period, and come up with the almost 220 million people NBC claims to have set the record with. This could have been done by FOX--when American Idol aired the same week as the 2008 Super Bowl, they could have taken ratings from Fox Reality Channel, Fox News, FX, Fox Sports, and their Websites, then over an 18 day period combined all of the viewers of all their shows and claim that they had the "most watched media company in TV history."

The truth is the 2008 summer Olympic average viewing numbers were almost one-fourth <u>lower</u> than in 1996 and were a huge 40% less than the giant ratings days of the 1970s. The NBC PR version spun it to make it look like it was the biggest Olympics in history--but that was to cover up the truth that it was much lower rated than many other Olympics!

It happened again with the 2012 games, where every media outlet reported "record ratings." But it just wasn't true. If you read NBC's wording carefully, it says the London Olympics were "the highest-rated Summer Games staged outside the U.S. since 1976." So there were higher-rated games before 1976? Higher-rated games held in the U.S.? Even higher-rated Winter Games? Yup! That doesn't make the 2012 numbers "record ratings," does it?

The network tried the old "most watched TV event in history" as well with 219 million people watching at least six minutes of the London Olympics. Well, what other "event" in history has ever run for 20 straight days, taking up 4 to 5 hours of prime time along with hundreds of hours of daytime coverage on multiple networks? The answer is: none! So, yes, NBC was the most-watched "event" to meet those criteria—but it was also the ONLY television event to ever do that!

Something similar happened with the 2012 Super Bowl, where media headlines claimed it was the "highest-rated TV show in history." That is 100% false. As you read earlier, a "rating" involves the percentage of homes or people watching. And the 2012 Super Bowl had 47.8% of the people watching on average. It wasn't even the highest-rated Super Bowl of all time, which was the 1982 game at 49.1%. (At the left the online media darling Huffington Post didn't quite get the story right—so don't believe everything you read!)

The 2012 Super Bowl was actually only the fourth-highest rated game of all time and the ninth-rated overall show in TV history. Almost no one reported the truth that the game didn't set records when put into historical context. The *Newsday* article shown here was one of the few.

Other publications reported that the game was the "most watched program in television history," beating the record long held by the final episode of M*A*S*H. That is what I'd call a half-truth: it's true as far as it goes but it doesn't put it in any context.

The problem is that the country has grown by over 100 million people since the first Super Bowl. So of course more total people are going to tune in to it each year--there are more people in America each year! What's most surprising is that no matter how many people are added to the population, the percentage of people who watch the game stays pretty much the same every year!

The only fair comparison for TV ratings is the percentage of viewers that are watching a show. Here are the real numbers:

- M*A*S*H's final episode in 1983 had about 105.97 million viewers of the 234 million people in the country. That's 45% of all Americans at the time. It had 60.2% of the 83.3 million homes with televisions.
- Super Bowl XLIV in 2012 averaged 111.3 million viewers of the 313 million people in the country. That's 35% of all Americans today. It had 47.8% of the 114 million homes with television.

You tell me which numbers are better? M*A*S*H had 45% of the American population in 1983 vs. 35% for the Super Bowl in 2012. It had 60% of the homes in 1983 vs. 48% of the homes for football in 2012.

Add to that the fact that there is margin of error in every ratings estimate. So since the Super Bowl had an estimated 111 million total viewers compared to M*A*S*H's 106 million, either one could really be about 108 or 109 million so the "winner" is just too close to call. The measuring devices are also different today with modern people meters giving more detailed information than the diaries did in the 1980s.

All one can really conclude in this battle is that only about one-third of all Americans watched the 2012 game on average, which is a large number for any television show, and that most of the media bought the "highest rated" hype without putting it in perspective.

Sports numbers aren't the only ratings that get distorted. When Michael Jackson died in the summer of 2009, cable networks did around-the-clock coverage. Though there was a small spike in viewership levels, public interest waned quickly. The day before Jackson's memorial service, the news networks predicted that "hundreds of thousands" of fans were expected outside the Staples Center. Larry King even guessed "a million" and then claimed "billions" worldwide would be watching on TV. The real numbers: only 1,000 showed up outside the private service and 31 million total watched on 18 American television networks.

Even then the media didn't stop overstating the story—they tried to claim the Jackson funeral was one of the highest-rated TV events of all time. But not only was it nothing special in the ratings (about as many people watched the Jackson memorial as watched the final episode of American Idol that year), even in comparison to other funerals it didn't have as many TV viewers those held for Princess Diana or Ronald Reagan.

When ER left the air in 2009, its final episode drew only 16.4 million viewers. That was lower that week than NCIS, The Mentalist, Dancing with the Stars—and eight million fewer than American Idol. It was even lower rated than the finale of The Bachelor a few weeks earlier. For all the build-up to the hit medical show's final episode, with magazine covers and major interviews, the 16.4 million audience was a giant disappointment.

How was the NBC PR machine going to spin that one? They claimed "it was the biggest audience for a drama series finale since Murder She Wrote." Never mind that ER had lost 2/3 of its audience since the series' biggest episode (50 million watched when George Clooney saved a boy in pouring rain during the second season). Or that Will & Grace had a couple million more viewers for its finale on the same network three years earlier (but that's not a drama so that doesn't count to NBC's PR people).

NBC had to ignore every other major show finale for the previous 15 years (Seinfeld had 76 million, Friends 52 million, Home Improvement 35 million, even That '70s Show had 24 million!) to come up with a statement that made the ER finish sound record-breaking. It wasn't—it sputtered out so badly that it was shocking that it didn't even beat a couple of reality shows that week.

The same was true for the finale of Lost. The science fiction drama had been promoting its final episode for three years. ABC actually "cancelled" the show in 2007, giving a deadline to wrap up the storylines by 2010. So everyone knew the big finale was coming.

When it got to that week, the network went overboard to make sure everyone knew about the Lost finale. There were covers of *TV Guide* and *Entertainment Weekly*, giant articles in *USA Today* and other major papers. ABC repeated the first episode the night before the finale. They ran a two-hour retrospective just before the final episode aired. Jimmy Kimmel did a special reunion talk with the stars after the finale.

And then the ratings came in--the final episode got 13.9 million viewers. And a 7.5% household rating. That's it. A little more than 4% of the population watched.

That made it pretty much a disaster compared to all the

hype surrounding it. Placing it in the context of all the major finales in television history, it ranked 55th on the list of total viewers. Just below Mr. Belvedere and Wings.

MOST WATCHED FINALES

Ranked by Percentage of American Homes Watching

1.	M*A*S*H	60.2%
2.	The Fugitive	45.9
3.	Cheers	45.5
4.	Seinfeld	41.3
5.	Magnum P.I.	32.0
6.	Friends	29.8
7.	Cosby Show	28.0
8.	All in the Family	26.6
9.	Dallas	22.0
10.	Family Ties	20.8

So how did ABC spin Lost's low ratings? The episode "won its time slot." Well, that's true. It did beat every other show against it that night—many of the other networks didn't air anything worth beating because they feared a huge Lost audience. ABC also said that the episode had two million more viewers than the season's 11.5 million average. That's a positive, I guess, but nothing extraordinary.

The network then proclaimed Lost "was the week's top-rated scripted series among young adults." Okay, two episodes of American Idol beat it in young adults but that show's not scripted. So using that technicality ABC took the #3 show in the 18-49 year old bracket and made it the top series for that week.

Something similar happened with the 2012 finale of Desperate Housewives, which had only 11.1 million viewers. Headlines screamed "ratings winner" and "the show's highest ratings of the season," yet the series had lost two-thirds of the viewers it had for the final episode of its first season on the air, when over 30 million people watched!

The spin machine was going in full force when Larry King celebrated his 25th anniversary on CNN in 2010. Since his ratings had fallen so dramatically over the years (from 1.6 million in 1998 to an average 674,000 in 2010), the cable network had to find a way to make him sound more influential than he was. So they went to the Guinness Book of World Records and had Larry King Live proclaimed "The longest running TV show hosted by the same person on the same network and in the same time slot."

They sent out the press releases and virtually every major story about King's 2010 retirement reported that King hosted "the longest-running TV talk show of all time." The problem is that the way it was reported made it not true—he didn't host the longest-running talk show. King hosted the program for just over 25 years, while Johnny Carson hosted The Tonight Show on NBC for 29 years and 8 months. CNN would probably claim that the Tonight Show had different hosts of the Tonight Show before and after Carson, so that doesn't count.

Phil Donahue hosted a daytime talk show for 29 years, but that was in syndication and wasn't in the same time slot across the country. The same with Oprah and Mike Douglas. David Letterman has hosted a late night show for close to 30 years but on two different networks. So CNN's PR move was misleading at best, deceptive at worst. And something that the media completely bought into without question.

The spin may not always come from the network press releases but may reflect the political or social agenda of the entertainment writers. There's no better example than the coverage of President Barack Obama and his first prime time press conference in March of 2009. Every outlet reported that he had scored "big numbers." Combining all the networks that aired it (including cable), 29.5 million people watched. *Entertainment Weekly* even claimed he was the "top program of the week."

The problem is that press conferences are news events and not programs, airing without commercials so they don't officially show up in the Nielsen report. His conference was also aired on multiple networks, so it wasn't a single program on a single network. Reporters claiming how "big" the numbers were ignored the fact that the Obama ratings were lower than similar press conferences with Bill Clinton and Ronald Reagan. No record was set and the viewership wasn't as large as the media wanted you to believe.

Another example of this was the Tiger Woods scandal and his return to playing golf in 2010. Woods' decision to come out of hiding to play the Masters caused a media frenzy. Since he not only was the world's top-ranked golfer but previously had been America's most admired athlete, the press knew that covering his return to the game would bring big viewing levels.

We know they thought that because they kept telling us that it was going to break records! The media said it would be the "highest-rated Masters of all time" and might even be "the most-watched TV event in history." The Nielsen Company itself wrote a pre-tournament release with historical data that said Woods' return "could make this year's Masters a record-breaking event."

Entertainment Weekly predicted that "Woods' presence, should he qualify for weekend play, will likely boost ratings to well above the previous one-day golf record of 20.3 million viewers, set during Woods' first masters victory in 1997." They even predicted, "the final tally could top 25 million—a figure on par with an NFL playoff game."

Then came reality. The day Tiger returned to the fairway, ESPN's rating was 3.4% with 4.9 million viewers. That's it. A major disappointment that should have embarrassed all of the writers who predicting big numbers but *Broadcasting* magazine actually wrote that Tiger was "providing monster ratings." Another publication said his appearance "saved golf."

Sorry, but 4.9 million is a long way from 20 million. And by the second day it had dropped to 3.9 million. The tournament got beat that week in the sports ratings by WWE Raw!

CBS had its spin-mode ready for the mediocre weekend numbers. They said it was the "highest rated Masters in nine years" and "the third-highest final round of any golf tournament since 1986." That may all be true, but the viewership came nowhere near the pre-tournament predictions and were nowhere close to records. The headlines should have said that Tiger's return failed to draw the expected audience.

The same thing happened when the US Soccer team made the top 16 in the 2010 World Cup. Headlines proclaimed that America had finally fallen in love with the sport, with *USA Today* predicting "big TV ratings," while another said the numbers were "through the roof." The Associated Press even predicted that the team's game against Ghana "could top the U.S. national team record."

The reality was that the match earned an 8.2 rating, which means eight percent of the homes in America watched. Those are very strong numbers for soccer, but nowhere near record-breaking (the 1994 Italy-Brazil final drew higher ratings in America!). Even the 2010 Spain-Netherlands finale had about twice as many viewers as the American match at a viewing percentage was lower than some previous years.

The overall 2010 World Cup ratings on cable were .2—that's 2/10's of one percent of the homes, the same as the previous two World Cups. And the actual cable household viewership per game was down. When you added in the higher-rated ABC games, the overall average rating for all matches was 2.1% of the homes and 3.8 million viewers. That's a little over 1% of the population.

Instead of proclaiming that it was proof of a resurgence in soccer in America, the headlines should have said that there is still little interest in the sport. While columnists wrote that the 2010 World Cup was proof that American viewers were finally embracing soccer, context would have shown that the overall numbers were flat or even dropped.

It has happened multiple times in recent years when every media outlet (including radio's Rush Limbaugh) reported the "record ratings" of NFL games. One ESPN commentator even claimed pro football games were getting their "biggest ratings ever." But despite the fact that ratings were indeed up for some games, they were actually down overall in some averages and merely "the largest audience for any regular-season primetime NFL telecast in 15 years."

Oh—so no record was set. The numbers used to be higher in the 1990s. These stories need factual context. Like the writer who headlined that a January 2012 Cowboys-Giants game was the "Most-Watched NBC Prime Time Game Ever." Wow—so that must prove today's ratings are higher than ever, right? One problem—NBC has only aired prime time games for six years. These numbers are still low compared to 30 years ago. And if you read deep into the story you find that the overall averages for the Sunday Night Football season were actually down!

Media writers often mistake a slight uptick in ratings as being "records" or "best ever" when they're not. The fact is most major sporting events on television today don't come close to the viewing levels achieved in the 1970s, '80s and '90s, before ESPN started airing games and competing sports networks were started.

It's too bad that when the predictions don't match expectations, the media won't come back and report the truth. The public is left with the misconception that viewing levels were "big" or "record-breaking" when often that's either not true or a distortion. You have to read the fine print.

Critical darling Mad Men typically gets less than one percent of the population watching but writers and industry executives love it (which is why it earned the Best Drama Emmy Award a record four years in a row). The final episode of the 2012 season brought "record high ratings" according to stories. CBS News reported that the season finale "set a ratings record" with 2.7 million viewers. But it simply wasn't true. The fifth season premiere just two months earlier had 3.5 million viewers!

How could the press make such an obvious mistake? In their hyperventilating about the program they misread the AMC press release that said Mad Men had its highest-rated final episode of any season of the show. And that's true. But that was still down 25% from the number that watched the first episode that year. Oh.

So don't believe all the hype about a show like Mad Men. Put it into the perspective that about 99% of the population does not watch the show.

Another recent example is the 2012 History Channel mini-series Hatfields and McCoys. It shocked the popular press by drawing relatively large numbers for a cable show, peaking at over 14 million viewers for the final episode.

The folks at History Channel spun the numbers into calling it the "most-watched non-sports event in advertiser supported cable history." That's technically true, but pick that statement apart to realize that it was not the most-watched show in cable history. It didn't do as well in the ratings as a number of NFL games on ESPN and didn't come close to Disney Channel's High School Musical 2, which had over 17 million viewers. Disney Channel doesn't air ads so that record is ignored by The History Channel, which is "advertiser supported cable."

Unfortunately most the media don't read press releases carefully and instead spun the story to be "Hatfields and McCoys set cable record" and "History Channel has most-watched show in cable history." Neither of those statements are true but if you Google search stories about the mini-series that's what you'll find. That misinformation now remains online as fact even though the program did not set a cable record nor was the most-watched show. The best that can be said is that it was the highest-rated scripted cable show since High School Musical 2.

So when it comes to reading or hearing about TV ratings, be skeptical. "Big," "hit," "best," "cult favorite" or "the most since" are words used to hype shows that often are lower-rated, while there are other programs that receive little coverage attracting more viewers.

Chapter Three Discussion Questions

1. Explain how accurate ratings are.
2. How do people meters work?
3. Explain the types of numbers Nielsen reports.
4. How is Nielsen like an umpire?
5. How has Nielsen caused confusion by changing how ratings are reported? How do the media spin ratings?
6. What did Nielsen do in 2007? Explain the "live plus" ratings.
7. What's C3?
8. How does a cable network have two different ratings numbers?
9. Who isn't included in the rating viewership estimates?
10. What shows have the most total viewers that tune in for even a few minutes?
11. Explain the spin on the ratings for:
- 2008 Olympics
- Super Bowl (vs. M*A*S*H)
- Michael Jackson's death
- Show finales
- Larry King's "record"
- President Obama's first press conference
- Tiger Woods' return to the Masters
- The 2010 World Cup
- Hatfields and McCoys

Chapter Four

WHAT MAKES A HIT?

When the highest-rated non-sports series on television today attracts less than 12% of the households and averages 7% of the population watching, it may want to change its name to "A Small Portion of America's Idol."

Although the singing competition was the number one show on TV for seven years and was still number two in 2012, its Nielsen ratings must be placed into historical context. While it may be a success by today's standards, it has only one-third the percentage of homes watching compared to past top series. And there is no show on prime time television today, including football, that regularly attracts the number of viewers that used to watch 30 years ago.

Your reaction may be, "What? Are you trying to claim that old shows were more popular than Family Guy and Glee? That can't be!" If you have bought into the media hype, you'd swear that current "hits" are much more popular than older series that you've never heard of. But it's just not true.

Gunsmoke attracted 37.3 percent of the homes in 1960, Bonanza was on top with 36.3 in 1965, and Laugh-In hit 31.6 in 1969. Compare those numbers to more recent series—Grey's Anatomy's best numbers peaked at 12.5 percent of all homes, Desperate Housewives at 14.5, House at 11.1 and Sunday Night

Football with 12.9. That means recent popular programs have reached only about one-third of the homes as did past hits.

The common misperception is that today's "hits" are more popular than ever, but the opposite is true. For example, The Beverly Hillbillies is the highest-rated comedy of all time, reaching an average 39.1% of the homes in 1964. Cosby Show was almost as popular with 34.9% in 1987.

Today's top sitcom, Big Bang Theory, is watched in only 8% of the households. That's less than one-fourth the percentage of homes that watched Hillbillies or Cosby.

Even in terms of number of total viewers watching, Big Bang gets around 12 million while up to 60 million people watched Beverly Hillbillies when it peaked in 1964, beating some of the Super Bowls! And the population has grown by over 100 million!

Virtually no weekly television show on the air today is a hit if you use previous television standards. Back in the days of only three networks, a major hit was a prime time series that got at least 20 to 30 percent of the homes in America watching. You needed at least a 20 rating to be a top 20 show.

Now a popular broadcast prime time series only needs 6 to 12 percent of the homes to watch, and there are series making the top 20 with only a 4 or 5 rating! The way a "hit" is defined gets revised every year as viewers have more networks to choose from and ratings drops for the top-rated shows.

The threshold first changed when cable networks expanded in the 1980s and the broadcast networks began losing viewers. As you can see in the chart below, the numbers started to drop quickly and, other than a slight resurgence with The Cosby Show, it was all downhill from there.

NIELSEN PRIME TIME RATINGS COMPARISON

These are the #1 shows of the year since the start of valid ratings in 1960, with their household rating for the season (the percentage of homes watching). On the right are the number of top 25 shows each year with an average rating of over 20%, which used to be the minimum needed to be considered a "hit" to stay on the air.

1960-61	Gunsmoke	37.3%	25+
	Wagon Train	32.1	25+
	Beverly Hillbillies	36.0	25+
	Beverly Hillbillies	39.1	25+
	Bonanza	36.3	25+
1965-66	Bonanza	31.8	25+
	Bonanza	29.1	25+
	Andy Griffith	27.6	25+
	Laugh In	31.8	25+
	Laugh In	26.3	25+
1970-71	Marcus Welby	29.6	24
	All in the Family	34.0	25
	All in the Family	33.3	24
	All in the Family	31.2	25
	All in the Family	30.2	25

1975-76	All in the Family	30.1	25
	Happy Days	31.5	25
	Laverne & Shirley	31.6	25
	Laverne & Shirley	30.5	25
	60 Minutes	28.4	25
1980-81	Dallas	34.5	22
	Dallas	28.4	19
	60 Minutes	25.5	13
	Dallas	25.7	15
	Dynasty	25.0	9
1985-86	Cosby Show	33.7	14
	Cosby Show	34.9	10
	Cosby Show	27.8	9
	Cosby Show	25.6	7
	Cosby Show	23.1	6
1990-91	Cheers	21.3	2
	60 Minutes	21.9	1
	60 Minutes	21.9	2
	60 Minutes	20.9	2
	Seinfeld	20.6	2

1995-96	ER	22.0	2
	ER	20.7	2
	Seinfeld	20.5	2
	ER	17.8	0
	Who/Millionaire	18.9	0
2000-01	Survivor	17.4	0
	Friends	18.4	0
	CSI	16.3	0
	CSI	15.9	0
	CSI	16.5	0
2005-06	American Idol	17.6	0
	American Idol	17.3	0
	American Idol	16.1	0
	American Idol	15.1	0
	American Idol	13.7	0
2010-11	American Idol	14.5	0
2011-12	Sunday Night Football	12.9	0

These numbers show that there are no longer any "hits" on television if measured by the old traditional definition of needing to have at least 20% of the homes in America watching. The two major ratings declines came in 1981-82 (after cable networks started and pulled viewers away, like ESPN in 1979 and CNN in 1980) and in 1987-88 (when the Nielsen company changed to the people meters, which lowered network viewing numbers).

These are just the prime time numbers. When you get to daytime, late night and cable networks the audiences get much smaller. The media end up calling almost anything a "hit" that seems trendy or that critics like. Often that word is generated by the network PR people.

For example, a 2010 FOX drama called Lone Star was picked by critics as the best new series of the upcoming season. Then it premiered in 85th place with only 4.1 million viewers. Yet the network ran promotional ads calling Lone Star "the new TV season's big hit." After a week of trying to generate "buzz" about the show, its second episode dropped to 3.3 million viewers and was instantly cancelled by the network that had just claimed it was a "hit."

That same year another network ran online previews of what it called "the hit ABC show My Generation" just one day before the series was canned after coming in 71st place with 5.1 million viewers.

The CBS sitcom How I Met Your Mother has been called a "hit" with "boffo numbers" (*Daily Variety*). It only had 9.6 million average viewers in 2012 and was 44th in the ratings. It had fewer viewers than now-cancelled series Rules of Engagement and Terra Nova.

So why is it called a hit? One reason is that it stars media darling Neil Patrick Harris and has a cast filled with young people. Another is that for a long time it had the lowest median age (44) of any CBS prime time series. It does do well in the young adult demographic (placing 17th) but the media somehow missed the story that there are virtually the same number of young adults watching NCIS, a show that gets very little press attention because of its older cast.

Glee was called a "hit series" by *USA Today*, "a ratings hit from the get-go" by *Daily Variety* magazine, "the industry's biggest story of the year," "the TV sensation" in *Entertainment Weekly* and a "bona-fide hit" by *Advertising Age*, yet it only attracted an average of 9.9 million viewers (3% of the population) and came in 35th place in its first season.

Broadcasting magazine went so far as to call Glee "the season's biggest freshman hit" and *Variety* called it the "season's hottest new hour" but that simply wasn't true. NCIS: LA also was a first-year series that year and came in 9th in the ratings, making it far-and-away a bigger freshman success story. The Good Wife, Undercover Boss and Castle were also actual first-season hour-long hits that got higher ratings than Glee. Yet most of the publicity went to the politically-correct hip musical.

If you want to argue that Glee attracted a young audience, it was beaten by Dancing with the Stars in adults 18-49! And while Glee set musical download records, it sold fewer actual albums than Hannah Montana and High School Musical.

Even on the FOX network it didn't do as well as Bones or House. The fact that often goes unreported is that Glee lost 60% of American Idol's viewers when the two programs aired back-to-back. That is considered a huge loss of lead-in audience. By late

June of 2010, without Idol in front of it, Glee reruns ranked 60th one week and 64th the next, with only had 4.1 and 3.9 million viewers. It was beat by Spanish-language Hasta Dinero Separe on Univision!

When Glee came back in the fall of 2010, it scored 13.5 million viewers with a special appearance by Britney Spears and the media went into overdrive again. *Entertainment Weekly* actually reported that Glee "became the first show in 17 years to build upon its season-premiere performance." Not only was that a complete fabrication, but seven different shows that very week accomplished this same "record" that Glee set. Even Undercover Boss built on its season premiere numbers—two days before the Glee episode!

The musical had become the media darling and nothing was going to stop writers from trying to make it seem like a hit the size of Seinfeld. *TV Guide* put the show's producer on the top of the list of "The 25 Most Influential People in Television." And in the summer of 2010, one TV publication speculated that Glee could become the number one show on the tube in 2010-2011!

So what happened? The show's ratings started to drop. By 2012 it was down to 56th place with only 8.7 million viewers. Musical sales almost disappeared. And critics started to complain that the series was contrived and repetitive.

Often a once-popular series will continue to be called a "hit" long after started dropping in the ratings. For four seasons the island series Lost was a true success, placing in the top 20 and peaking with 15.7 million viewers. It wasn't doing American Idol-size numbers but it held a strong audience for a long period. But during the last two seasons it dropped out of the top 25 and ended its final year with only 11.6 million watching an average episode.

In its final season *Daily Variety* was still calling it "a potent ratings performer" and "an impressive showing." Sorry, but getting less than 4% of the people in the country to watch isn't very "potent." Media writers often refuse to accept reality for shows they like and will often overstate a program's popularity based on past success, as they have done for years with The Simpsons and Family Guy.

Compare Lost's praise to press coverage of American Idol that same season, which was still number one but the media were claiming that viewers were "losing interest" and that the program "no longer drew big numbers." *Daily Variety* even started a front-page story after the show's 2010 finale with, "Can American Idol be saved?" (which *TV Guide* later repeated twice with articles such as "Can The New Judges Save American Idol?"). Saved from what? It was the number one show on television—not exactly destined for cancellation!

Daily Variety's writer claimed the 2010 season-ending Idol episode "felt more like a wake than a finale" and suggested the network consider pulling the plug on the series! Then the next season the ratings went up!

Reporters knock down those on top that they don't like (especially reality shows) and overpraise the underdogs that they love. Writers will spin a story to make it more dramatic even if it doesn't reflect an accurate picture of the truth. Idol was portrayed as a loser on its last breath while during the same season Lost was said to go out a winner—even though Idol had twice as many viewers and was the number one series on TV.

When *Time* magazine made the ridiculous claim that Lost "changed the way we watch television," even *Daily Variety*'s Brian Lowry called that "balderdash." He used an entire column to point out that although he enjoyed the show, claiming the series had any significance by ignoring the show's dropping ratings "says more about us media folk, frankly, than it does about TV." Thanks goodness there was one person in the press willing to tell the truth.

Lowry may be the only writer who seems to get it. When the *New York Times* wrote in the summer of 2010, "The nation is once again transfixed by Mad Men," Lowry responded that the newspaper was "apparently oblivious to the fact 99% of the nation doesn't watch the show." He said the *Times* calling the series a "phenomenal success" proves its "perceived impact echoes far beyond its audience size."

Another example of how the press reports on a television show's status is Jay Leno's prime time talk show. It ran five nights a week at 9 p.m. in 2009-2010 and its first episode had over 17 million viewers, making it the number three show on television for the week. After he placed four episodes in the top 20 that week Leno was proclaimed a "hit," although most critics didn't like the series.

Then the numbers started dropping and critics went from trumpeting it as the first success of the season to calling it a flop. The *TV Guide* network even named it the biggest fiasco in television history, worse than the Janet Jackson Super Bowl wardrobe malfunction.

The prime time NBC talk show really did bomb, with its best night on average being Tuesdays when it came in 85th place with six million viewers.

Yet two NBC comedies airing that same season, Community and Parks & Recreation, both got lower audience averages than Leno. They were renewed and were called "hits." The sitcoms are still running three years after the Leno mess, despite the fact that they get lower numbers than the talk show host did! In 2012 P&R came in 134th place and Community placed 144th! They each had only around four million viewers. Even in the 18-49 demographic Parks came in 82nd and Community 102nd!

How come Leno's show is called a "failure" and the lower-rated comedies are "hits"? Because media writers like the hip scripted series and want to promote the shows hoping to get more people to watch. It's as simple as that.

Many criteria could be used for television series to be considered "hits":

- Time period. A prime time hit today may need 12 million viewers in order for it to make the top 20, but broadcast series in other dayparts only needs a few million viewers to be considered successful. The Today Show gets about five million while The Tonight Show gets three to four million. Soap operas get two to four million. Ellen Degeneres and Jimmy Kimmel attract only a couple million viewers.

   Summer prime time episodes also need fewer viewers to be considered hits. America's Got Talent often gets less than ten million viewers to top the summer ratings. And to make the top 20 in the summer a show only needs about six million people watching.

- Demographics. The networks today claim that they don't need to win in "total households" or "total viewers" in order to be successful—they need to win in the adult 18-49 category. That's purportedly the group that advertisers want and many online sites only report ratings in that age range.

   So Family Guy is proclaimed a "hit" because it is the 21st most popular show in that age group (3.8 of the show's 4.8 million viewers fall into the 18-49 demographic). In 2012 the animated series placed 70th overall, lower than cancelled shows Scandal, GCB, Missing and How to Be a Gentleman.

A number of studies have shown that the younger demographic isn't necessarily the best audience for an advertiser. Some of the biggest moneymaking series on television actually appeal to the older demographic group that has money to spend. Networks still promote the misconception that older, rural viewers should be shunned in favor of younger, urban dwellers. And a number of media outlets now only report ratings information for the 18 to 49 age group!

- Ratings growth. Any program that shows an increase in audience is trumpeted for its growth, much like stock market gains. But when you hear about the amazing audience growth of a program, it may be because the ratings were significantly low to start with.

The CW network is a good example because all of its shows are on the bottom of the ratings chart. It needs to trumpet small successes whenever it can. So when long-running but low-rated One Tree Hill started its final season in 2011, the network was excited that the first episode was "up 26%." Wow—that's a huge gain, right?!

Then you look at the numbers more closely. The first episode did increase—from 1.4 million to 1.75 million. That's right—it got about another 350,000 viewers. But the series concluded with 1.43 million for the finale and ended up 180th out of 195 shows. Sorry, CW, but that's not a hit. It means almost no one was watching.

On the other hand, when a popular reality program's numbers go down, no matter how slightly, the press reports it as a tragedy. Virtually every article written about American Idol's 2012 season mentioned that the ratings were down and it had its lowest-rated finale ever. Yet it remained the number one non-sports series on television. Despite repeated stories that Idol was no longer a success it was actually still one of TV's biggest hits.

- Network. CBS had the most shows in the 2012 prime time top 20 while NBC had the fewest. The threshold for success at CBS is much higher than at NBC. So a program with lower ratings that CBS might cancel could actually be considered a "hit" on NBC.

A comparison of how that impacts network programming can be seen in Spring 2012's 7:30 Thursday time slot. The CBS comedy Rob, one of the most popular shows on television, came in 25th place but was cancelled. It aired behind Big Bang Theory on Thursday night and CBS expected more of the show. In the same time period NBC renewed Community in 144th place! It had few viewers but was a media darling (*TV Guide* put it on a "save the show" cover) with a vocal online fan base.

Rob's ratings were higher than any scripted show on NBC. But CBS cancelled it because networks have differing standards of what makes a hit. And it didn't help that Rob's theme (a Jewish guy marries into a Mexican-American family) was heavily criticized by media writers and minority groups—which embarrassed the reputation of CBS.

One of the fastest-growing networks in America is Univision, the only broadcast network that saw its overall numbers increase in 2012. There are weeks that the Spanish-language network's telenovelas get higher ratings than many of the other networks and it ended the season beating the CW in overall averages (3.6 million to 1.7 million). But you wouldn't know that by the media reports because the Univision numbers are not included in the end-of-season ratings summary!

- Cable. Since there are over 400 cable channels to divide up the viewing audience, the threshold for what is considered a success is much lower. A prime time cable series only needs about three million viewers to make the cable top 20, which is one-fourth what is needed for prime time broadcast network hit status.

The biggest cable programs are sporting events, reality shows and kids programs. Some score highly enough that they could rank in the top 30 of the weekly Nielsen reports. But cable ratings are released separately from the broadcast rankings. So when you see the weekly prime time chart from Nielsen, it doesn't include cable numbers. That means Jersey Shore's 8 million viewers might make it a top 20 show on the normal Nielsen ratings list, but it doesn't get placed there.

Many cable shows with small audiences are called "hits" because they do well on networks that traditionally don't get a lot of viewers. The pay channel Starz said it had a "hit" with a series called Party Down, which co-starred Glee's Jane Lynch, by attracting only 125,000 viewers.

In 2012 left-leaning political channel Current TV fired Keith Olbermann, who had only 177,000 viewers, even though the network had called it a "hit show" that was a "game changer." Current replaced him with Eliot Spitzer, who premiered with only 47,000 in the audience! Some cable systems are now considering dumping the cable channel because it isn't meeting minimum viewing levels.

- Stars. The media go wild over major movie stars that decide to do television series. A famous actor brings instant credibility to a new show and the press often calls the program with a star a "hit" before it even goes on the air.

For Oscar-nominated Glenn Close, her FX series Damages premiered to 3.7 million viewers, by the start of the second season it lost more than half of its audience. The reason the network brought it back? Probably the Emmy Awards it won and the publicity the star generated from media writers who called it a "hit."

HBO is able to get major stars to commit to TV series, such as the 2012 drama Luck that featured Academy Award winner Dustin Hoffman. Its first episode has just over a million viewers but by the seventh episode it was down to 474,000. When the network cancelled the series after three horses were killed during second season production, reporters wrote the sad story about "the HBO hit Luck." It not only was not a hit, it was a major flop for the embarrassed pay channel.

- Rerunability. That may not be a real word (it's used online so it must be real, right?), but it is meant to convey the ability of a series to rerun well. Leave it to Beaver and Brady Bunch didn't make the top 25 of the ratings when they are originally on prime time, but in syndicated reruns they have been hits, doing better than former #1 prime timers All in the Family, ER, and Cosby Show.

Sitcoms tend to rerun the best in syndication. Big Bang Theory is both a hit in prime time and in reruns on local stations, while Seinfeld repeats are still in the top 25 of syndicated shows 20 years after they first aired. But some network programs haven't become successful until they were viewed daily in syndication, such as The Office, Family Guy and How I Met Your Mother.

The Web also contributes to the ability of a program to become popular. Saturday Night Live segments get more viewers online than on NBC. One recent week a little-seen ABC Family series called Pretty Little Liars held five of the top ten slots on iTunes even though it has around two million viewers. In these cases reruns transform series that had low numbers for original airings into non-prime time hits.

- Copycatability. There's another unique word—but it means that a series is so successful that other programs pop up that copy it. For example, NBC's The Biggest Loser led to a variety of scripted and reality weight-loss series, such as Extreme Makeover: Weightloss Edition, Mike and Molly, Ruby, One Big Happy Family, Huge, Fat Camp, Celebrity Fit Club, Shedding for the Wedding and Dance You're A— Off.

  The Real Housewives of Orange County not only led to a variety of spin-offs, but then The Real Housewives of New Jersey resulted in shows focused on that state, such as Jersey Shore, Jerseylicious and Jersey Couture.

  Television copies successful films. The best recent example is the large number of dramatic vampire shows that have come out after the success of Twilight. Within two years vampires were the focus of True Blood, Moonlight, Vampire Diaries and The Gates.

  Sometimes the first program to tackle a concept isn't the most successful. Star Search, Popstars and Making the Band were singing competitions that aired before American Idol, but it took the addition of Simon Cowell to turn Idol into the biggest amateur singing hit. And that then led to America's Got Talent, Nashville Star, Celebrity Duets, X Factor, The Voice and Gone Country.

- Critical praise and awards. When entertainment writers or industry executives fall in love with a show, they call it a "hit" and don't let facts get in their way. Networks often leave programs on the air simply because the critics love them, hoping that enough good press will get the ratings to go up.

Media writers love to trumpet little-seen new programs as part of their journalistic philosophy of bringing underdog stories to the masses. So in 2011, four of the five programs nominated for Best Comedy by the Television Critics Association were low-rated programs that almost no one watches, such as Louie, Community and Parks and Recreation. (All shows that got renewed over higher-rated series.)

Fresh, edgy programs (like Modern Family and Game of Thrones) may do well but are overhyped because writers want to help move the medium in a new direction. The press will ignore older and higher-rated traditional programming (like NCIS), no matter how successful, because writers believe it's their job to get the average viewer to watch newer "quality" programs.

A number of publications produce "S.O.S." articles every April, asking readers to "Save Our Show." Producers now have come to look to critics for help in getting low-rated series renewed. NBC executive Jeff Ingold admitted that weaker programs like Community get renewed due to critical support.

"There wasn't a great ratings story for the show, but there was a lot of online chatter and critics standing up for the show," he said. "That helps in keeping a show strong in terms of how it's perceived by the network. Hearing from objective third parties can keep these shows alive while waiting for audiences to find them."

Note how he refreshingly admits to the comedy's low ratings and that the critics kept it alive. He also states clearly that being perceived as successful is more important than ratings reality. However, he's wrong to claim that critics are "objective." They have a lot of subjective interest in mind when putting together stories about "hit" shows that they know are being watched by few.

The Emmy Awards and the Golden Globes can also save a program if it's close to being cancelled. Broadcast networks have always kept lower-rated award-winning series on the air, such as The Office and 30 Rock (which holds the record for the most Emmy nominations for a comedy series in a single season with 22 in 2009). Now that cable networks are winning for programs like Mad Men and Breaking Bad, they keep the programs on the air to stand out from the hundreds of other channels.

Saturday Night Live holds the single-series record for the most Emmy nominations with a total of 142 as of 2011. Despite often low ratings and mediocre material, awards can keep such a series alive as a perceived hit when other indications are that it should be cancelled.

- Length on the air. As noted by SNL's 38-year history, if a series is on the air for more than a couple years it tends to be considered a hit. But length doesn't necessarily reflect a show's audience status.

The history of TV is filled with long-running series that cannot be considered hits based on ratings, such as '50s comedy Ozzie & Harriet that ran for 14 seasons. The program According to Jim ran for eight years but never placed higher than 44th in the season rankings and ranked 146th when it was renewed for a final year!

The most famous long-running prime time program that doesn't have the ratings to support its hit status is The Simpsons. The program barely made the top 30 of the ratings just a couple times in its early years, but for more than the past decade it has wallowed in the lower half of the rankings (75th place in 2012) while others around it with those same numbers are cancelled.

The Simpsons is now said to be television's longest-running scripted program because as of 2013 it has been on 24 seasons. It terms of sheer longevity, it is a success. It also remains popular in terms of buzz, critical praise and merchandising. But if the threshold is ratings then The Simpsons is not a "hit" and hasn't been for decades.

Law & Order ended in 2010 after 20 years, tying Gunsmoke for the longest-running drama, while its spin-off remains on the air. Other record-breaking prime time series as of 2013 include news magazine 60 Minutes (45 years), Monday Night Football (43), 20/20 (35), America's Most Wanted (25), Cops (24) and Real World (21).

The problem is that even the definition of how long a show has been on the air is changing. If you look up "longest running

U.S. prime time television series" on Wikipedia you find Hallmark Hall of Fame (which are a few specials a year, not series), Saturday Night Live (not a prime time show), National Geographic Explorer (specials on five different networks) and the seasonal ESPN football pre-game show! None of those fit the traditional standards regarding weekly prime time television.

Often the success of a show is measured not by years but by the number of "seasons" it aired. Traditionally the word season meant one year—but reality television has changed that. Now a TV season can range from 4 episodes to 52 episodes or more. Reality shows split their year into different seasons based on different casts, so Survivor can claim to have 26 seasons over a period of 13 years. The lack of a clear definition for season makes those numbers a flawed historical comparison.

In the early days of the medium a series usually aired 39 new episodes a year, with 13 weeks of summer repeats. In some cases the "live" shows of the early '50s aired a new episode every week of the year. Compare that to today's cost-saving production schedule where producers of scripted series crank out only 22 to 24 new episodes per season. Family Guy, over 11 seasons, has telecast fewer episodes than Leave It to Beaver broadcast in only six years in the 1950s!

A series is now often given credit for a full "season" even if it airs merely one pilot episode (as Seinfeld did in 1989) or runs for a few weeks in the summer (as did Seinfeld for four weeks in 1990) or starts in the middle of a television year (just as Seinfeld returned in January of 1991).

So compare each of the following TV sitcoms that are given credit for running "nine seasons":

- Seinfeld was on the air for seven and one-half calendar years, but summer and mid-year airings were counted as separate "seasons" to give it a total of nine! It had 180 episodes.
- Father Knows Best's original 203 episodes were only aired over a six-year period from 1954 to 1960, then CBS and ABC played prime time reruns of the show for three more years to give it a claim of nine seasons!
- Everybody Loves Raymond was on CBS every week for eight years and eight months with 210 episodes, getting it close to a true nine-season run.

So all three shows are said to have spent "nine seasons" on network television prime time despite the fact that one made new episodes for six years, one for seven and one-half years, and one for just under nine years.

The media confuse the issue by accepting whatever illogical definition of season a network wants to use. Sex & the City had 94 episodes in its "six season" run from 1998 to 2004, an average of 15 shows a year. That became a standard number for cable series like South Park or Nip/Tuck. (One studio executive said, "It's a lot easier to make 13 great episodes than it is to deliver 22 decent ones.") Others deliver even fewer each year, such as the HBO prison drama Oz only airing eight original episodes each "season." And the British PBS series Sherlock had only three episodes for its second "season" in 2012!

A better system of deciding which show is the longest-running would be to compare the number of episodes made. The record-holder is ESPN's SportsCenter, which hit the 50,000 episode mark in 2012.

When it comes to prime time, The Simpsons is always proclaimed as the longest-running entertainment show on today. It began its series run in January of 1990 (after a December 1989 Christmas special) and as of Spring 2012 had aired 508 episodes.

The dirty little media secret is that there is actually another comedy on television right now that has run longer than The Simpsons and often gets better ratings. America's Funniest Home Videos started as an ABC special one month before the animated series' Christmas show. AFV then premiered with host Bob Saget earlier the very same evening that The Simpsons started in 1990!

Funniest Home Videos has aired 583 episodes as of Spring 2012, more than the FOX animated show, and in 2012 ranked 86th, just a few notches lower than the Simpsons. Some weeks during the regular season Funniest Home Videos beat the Simpsons in the ratings. In April of 2012 AFV was #1 in adults 18-49 in its time slot—pretty good for a 22-year-old show!

Despite the fact that it has been on the air longer and aired more original episodes, the media fail to report AFV as beating The Simpsons as the longest-running prime time entertainment series because AFV did not air weekly in 2000. Instead it ran a series of home video specials hosted by comedians before returning to a regular time slot in 2001 with new host Tom Bergeron.

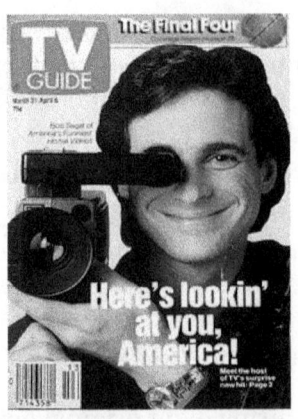

But TV history buffs should recall that The Simpsons also took a long time-out to allow writers to create new episodes. From 2000 to 2004, the animated series only ran six months of new shows each year instead of the normal nine months. The issue about who holds the record could be resolved by using the number of episodes as the standard instead of trying to measure uneven seasons.

Then there's King of the Hill, which claims to have run for 13 seasons since it aired from January 1997 to September 2009. But upon closer inspection, only 253 episodes ran, which is closer to 10 seasons of any other current series during that time period and would have been a little over six seasons compared to series from years ago. How can 253 episodes be 13 seasons?

Because King of the Hill did not air complete seasons and in the fall of 2005 (when it was originally cancelled by FOX before later receiving a reprieve) it twice went six weeks in the middle of the year without new episodes—airing only six new half-hours in a four-month period. History books will claim it ran longer than the 12 seasons of My Three Sons but the truth is that it only did so by running incomplete seasons, making nowhere near the 380 episodes that My Three Sons had.

The 2008 writers strike also messed up the season concept because series were interrupted in the middle of the year—some came back shortly after the strike ended, while others waited to play new episodes six to 12 months later. Lost had to cut its season short. The show 24 decided to stop trying to make a season that year and turned it into a TV movie. And some series went almost a year before a new episode was aired.

The concept of "season" has traditionally meant a show starts in the fall and ends original episodes in May. The Nielsen season numbers for prime time network series reflect those nine months. But networks try to make some shows stand out from the rest by changing when a season starts and stops. USA Network series Psych makes one season of shows but spreads them out over three different times of a calendar year, where the new episodes air for two months and then go into reruns again for a few months before the next part of the season pops up.

Reality shows like America's Next Top Model air multiple seasons (which it calls "cycles") in the same calendar year. The Tyra Banks-hosted competition started in May of 2003 and by the spring of 2012 had aired 18 "cycles" but it had only been on the air for nine years.

Survivor and Dancing with the Stars have one "season" in the fall and another "season" in the spring. It messes up the end-of-year ratings rankings because these reality shows air two "seasons" within one actual Nielsen ratings year. Some count them as separate shows with different casts, while others combine the two "seasons" ratings on the end-of-year list that comes out in May.

Compare that to ABC's hit game show Who Wants to Be a Millionaire, which ran four nights a week during one season and three nights a week during another. The series broadcast 363 episodes from 2000 to 2002, more than ER's 331 broadcasts over a 15-year period! But the record books say that Millionaire was only on for three seasons, making it one of the shorter-running hit television shows in history.

FLOPS

The opposite of the hit show is the flop, one that bombs in the ratings and is usually taken off the air quickly. Normally programmers become so impatient that they dump a low-rated program after just a few weeks.

About 15% of all television shows are true "hits," while at least 50% are flops. Some are cancelled so quickly that you don't even know they were on the air. Did you know Hugh Jackman starred in a TV series the same year he was in X-Men? It was a 2007 musical crime drama called Viva Laughlin on CBS and it was canned after two airings.

Other short-lived programs include reality shows The Will and The Princes of Malibu (featuring future Hills stars Spencer Pratt and Brody Jenner). Secret Talents of the Stars ran for one episode on CBS in 2008 and was cancelled, as were Anchorwoman on FOX and Quarterlife in NBC. The year before the same thing happened to Emily's Reasons Why Not, starring Heather Graham, on ABC.

There have even been cases where a program is made and then the network cancels it before it goes on the air. HBO produced six episodes of 12 Miles of Bad Road in 2008 at a cost of $25 million before it decided the program wasn't quality enough for the pay network to air.

Other programs that were made but you never saw include controversial reality show Welcome to the Neighborhood (where neighbors voted to kick families off the block), Seriously Dude I'm Gay, Jason Bateman in The Jake Effect, Randy Quaid's The Grubbs, Rewind with Scott Baio and Mark Burnett's life story as a sitcom called Commando Nanny along with his game show Jingles.

The most unusual string of show cancellations have come from NBC's Thursday night lineup. It was called "Must See TV" from 1982 to 2006 and included hits like Cosby Show, Family Ties, Mad About You, Frasier, Friends, Seinfeld and Will & Grace.

New shows were placed right after these hits and if the new program's ratings weren't quite up to the strong lead-in, the new series was gone—even if it was in the top ten of the ratings. Flops from NBC's "Must See" Thursday schedule include:

DEAR JOHN (88)	GRAND (90)
RHYTHM & BLUES (92)	MADMAN OF THE PEOPLE (94)
SINGLE GUY (95)	HOPE AND GLORIA (95)
NAKED TRUTH (97)	FIRED UP (97)
UNION SQUARE (97)	JESSE (98)
VERONICA'S CLOSET (98)	CURSED (00)
INSIDE SCHWARTZ (01)	GOOD MORNING MIAMI (02)
COUPLING (03)	FOUR KINGS (06)

And the notorious Friends spin-off JOEY (04)

So just as many shows failed as were successful on NBC's Thursday nights over a 20-year period, even though "Must See" Thursday has a reputation as being only success stories. The interesting aspect is that almost all of those failed series were on Nielsen's top ten list—so they would normally qualify as "hits." They were cancelled because they failed to retain at least 80 to 85% of the lead-in's audience.

For example, in 1998 a series called Union Square was ranked eighth but only lasted one season because it lost 20% of the audience in between Friends and Seinfeld.

Today a major loss of lead-in audience doesn't guarantee cancellation. Glee has stayed on the air while loosing 60% of American Idol's lead-in audience. Don't Trust the B in Apt. 23 was renewed in 2012 even though it lost over 40% of Modern Family's viewers.

The flop spin-off Joey premiered as the number one show on television. Then gradually over the next few months people stopped watching and it was cancelled after its second season. That's called **having no legs**, which means that the series was like a marathon runner that ran out of steam after only a mile or two.

Some of these were proclaimed "pop culture hits" or "cult hits" but went downhill after an initial surge, such as Heroes, The O.C. and Gossip Girls. Networks stick with them for a few years hoping to revive interest in a show that had first-year success.

There is often no sense to what shows network executives cancel and which ones they stick with for a few years. Series like Seinfeld, Cheers, Everybody Loves Raymond, M*A*S*H, JAG and The Biggest Loser were all initially low rated and some even taken off the air for months, but someone at the network saw something in them that they stuck with until the shows became successful.

Other flop programs get resurrected after they have been cancelled. The most famous example of this was King of the Hill, which had been off the air for over a year and was only airing in reruns on FOX—until it was paired with Family Guy on Sunday nights and the ratings started to dramatically increase. So the network had to renegotiate all the contracts and bring everyone back to make new episodes. The same happened with Futurama, which was off the air five years before Comedy Central revived it in 2010 under contentious money negotiations with the voice cast.

The Surreal Life was on the WB network for one year in 2003, with two different sets of celebrities. Then it was dropped, only to be picked up a year later by VH1 and turned into a huge cultural hit. The program led to a large number of spin-offs, including Strange Love, Flavor of Love, Fame Games, My Fair Brady and indirectly I Love New York. In all there are at least seven TV series that can be traced back to the Surreal Life's VH1 success—which means if it would have stayed cancelled you never would had the chance to see the romantic adventures of Flavor Flav!

There are even certain performers that have a pattern of being in shows that are flops. Tom Arnold, Bonnie Hunt and Jason Bateman are among those whose casting regularly poisoned the potential for the new series in which they co-starred.

Simon Baker may have been an "overnight success" due to the immediate popularity of his series The Mentalist in 2008, but he had already been in two recent flops on the same network (a series called Smith in 2006 and The Guardian in the early 2000s). CBS knew he was star material and kept trying.

Then there's George Clooney—you think of him as a movie star who started on television in ER. But he spent decades around Hollywood making many series that flopped (Bodies of Evidence, Baby Talk, the sitcom E/R) or being fired after only working a season or two on others (The Facts of Life, Roseanne).

The "queen" of failed television series is none other than Betty White. She started on television in 1949 (and actually was used as a model to test the first TV signals in 1939). She is often remembered for her Emmy-winning work on Golden Girls (which ran for seven years) and Mary Tyler Moore Show (where she appeared in 39 episodes during the final four seasons). As of this writing she is still working at age 90 and has won seven Emmy Awards. She was nominated 20 times, including the first woman to win an Emmy as best game show host and a 2010 win at age 88 for guest hosting Saturday Night Live.

What the media like to overlook are her many television flops. They include Life With Elizabeth (12 episodes starting in 1953), Date with the Angels (33 episodes, 1957), The Betty White Show (14 episodes, 1977), Just Men (daytime game show that lasted three months in 1983), The Golden Palace (24 episodes, 1992), Maybe This Time (18 episodes, 1995) and The Ladies Man (30 episodes, 1999).

Everyone seems to love Betty White today, but she also may hold some type of record for guest starring in the largest number of famous TV failures. From Lucas Tanner and Ellery Queen in the 1970s to Love Sydney and Hotel in the 1980s. She appeared on Bob Newhart's only modern sitcom flop, on Carol Burnett's failed Carol & Company, and in an Alf television movie. Her guest star trail includes Nurses, LA Doctors, Ellen's 2001 sitcom failure, Everwood, Providence, the animated bomb Father of the Pride and even the infamous Friends spin-off Joey! Betty White is now considered TV royalty, but in truth she's the queen of cancelled television shows.

Chapter Four Discussion Questions

1. How have the numbers used to define a prime time hit changed over the years? How do ratings for current shows compare to past programs?
2. Are shows today more popular than ever? Explain.
3. What does the chart of #1 shows reveal about the change in viewership numbers over the years?
4. Explain why you should be skeptical of media coverage of shows like How I Met Your Mother or American Idol.
5. What "hit" shows got the same ratings numbers as Jay Leno's prime time flop? What does that tell you about media spin?
6. Explain how the following can impact how a show is considered a hit:
   - Time period
   - Demographics
   - Network
   - Cable
   - Stars
   - Rerunability
   - Copycatability
   - Critical praise & awards
   - Length on the air
7. How has the definition of a TV "season" changed?
8. What is a better way to compare shows instead of seasons?

9. Explain what comedy is actually longer running than The Simpsons.
10. What are examples of shows that were low rated at first but eventually became hits?
11. Why were so many Thursday night series cancelled?
12. What does it mean for a program to "have no legs"?
13. What stars have had flops? Who is the queen of cancelled shows?

Chapter Five

CENSORSHIP

Many viewers think they live in a society where they can watch whatever they want. Television has become a "right" in the minds of Americans because most of them pay to subscribe to cable channels. They think that if they pay for it then no one else should be able to "censor" what they watch.

But they don't get to "watch whatever they want" and don't understand the way television operates. Censorship occurs daily in two ways.

First, the government licenses a limited number of broadcast stations and the FCC is charged with making sure that all citizens' rights are considered by over-the-air broadcasters. Because not everyone can own a TV station (since channel space is so limited), Congress and courts have upheld that the government can enforce guidelines regarding television. The airwaves belong to the public, so public representatives can enforce boundaries in the public interest.

Second, network executives make decisions every day that impact what you do and do not see on TV. You don't actually make the decisions—they do. You are allowed to select from what they offer, but unless stations are willing to play a program (or make it available online) you don't get the choice to see it. That means there are times they will choose to not air something that you would like to watch, taking away your freedom.

Most networks and local stations are businesses that program what will attract an audience to make them money, much like a grocery store will carry items that it thinks will draw in customers. The supermarket has a right to decide if it wants to carry items that some customers may find objectionable (condoms, cigarettes, liquor) but they don't usually carry other items that are considered inappropriate for a family store (bong pipes, *Playboy* magazine). So, too, television networks have to decide what programs they will carry that will please their customers.

Networks can't air everything to please everybody, just as a grocery store can't stock every possible item available. A channel has to decide if a racy reality show will attract more viewers than a gory procedural drama. Viewers aren't even aware of the thousands of decisions networks make that keep people from seeing things, from the rejected pitch idea to the unaired pilot to the rejected infomercial.

Every season networks don't let you see 99% of the new program ideas that producers come up with. At one conference that I attended, FOX executives told of how they were pitched the idea of a new animated comedy featuring a family of gay dinosaurs. The rejection of that idea could be considered a form of censorship but broadcasters have traditionally seen their role as responsible gatekeepers for the community. They had every right to reject the idea based on what they perceived appropriate for their networks.

The only right you really have as a viewer is to select which network you trust to be the gatekeeper of your programming wishes. If you like chick flicks, you trust Lifetime. If you want to watch mixed martial arts, you look for it on Spike. For children's' programming parents have to decide if they want to trust public television, Disney Channel or Nickelodeon.

The point is that every network "censors" by selecting what they put on the air and you have to trust that they are programming what they think you will like. ESPN doesn't air all of the possible sports it could telecast—as a matter of fact it has contracts with professional and collegiate groups that allow many games to go to waste because the network chooses to not put them on. You may want to watch women's lacrosse and ESPN has the rights to it, but the network doesn't air the sport because it wouldn't attract enough viewers.

Movie channels like AMC or Turner Classics have thousands of films in their libraries that they rarely or never air. Isn't that censorship? MTV chooses which music videos to play in between their shows and rejects many of the artist's songs that are submitted. Censorship? The NBC Nightly News picks which news stories it thinks you would be interested in, while refusing to air stories about much of what is going on in the world. Censorship?

HBO has more leeway because it's a special pay channel that can air uncut R-rated movies because it doesn't have to follow strict FCC rules. Public TV has less leeway because much of its money comes from the government and donors, who may pull funding if there is something inappropriate. But in every case the viewer has no real say in what is being programmed—the networks are selecting what to offer you and rejecting many things that you will never see.

Isn't that censorship? Isn't that against the First Amendment's right to "free speech"?

Broadcast networks send their programming to local stations that are licensed by the FCC. Licensed stations are required to operate in the "public interest, convenience and necessity" and you can't just start your own station. You as a citizen have no "right" to use a station to broadcast what you want and they have no requirement to allow you on the air. So your "free speech" rights do not include broadcasting.

Cable systems are franchised by local governments and the FCC authorizes satellite companies to operate. You cannot just start your own cable or satellite company without some type of government approval, and certainly cannot have free access to any of the airtime on private cable networks. That means you don't have any "right" to free cable or satellite speech either.

You can communicate your desires to stations or networks and if you don't like what they air you can refuse to watch or stop supporting the sponsors. But to claim that you have some type of free speech right to decide what airs on television is a misunderstanding of the First Amendment.

Your free speech right is to pressure a station or network to change its business practices in order to air what you would like to see or to let others know what you think about a program. Some people want more family-oriented content and object when inappropriate material pops up on the screen, such as the Janet Jackson incident at the 2004 Super Bowl. Others want more "freedom" on channels that they watch and, like NYPD Blue producer Steven Bochco, want to put more profanity, sex and violence into programs to make them more "realistic."

Everyone has the right to peacefully communicate their preferences to stations, networks and other citizens. Those communications, ranging from emails and show-saving Websites to organized protests and advertiser boycotts, may or may not result in a change. But over time the medium does adjust its standards of what is appropriate because society's norms evolve.

What offended people in the past seems comical today. The history of the medium is filled with examples of censorship that ranges from silly to shocking:

- In 1952, Lucy could not say "pregnant," but had to use the word "expecting."
- In 1957, Elvis was appearing on Ed Sullivan when they took the shot only from the waist up and refused to show his hips swaying.
- 1950s sitcoms would show married couples sleeping in separate single beds, including real-life married couples like Ozzie & Harriet and Lucy & Desi.
- The '50s Chesterfield variety show sponsored by Chesterfield cigarettes demanded that stars couldn't say "Boy, that was lucky" because the company's major competitor was Lucky Strikes cigarettes.
- In 1963, Bob Dylan was to sing an anti-war song on Ed Sullivan. When the censors refused, he walked off the show.
- In 1966, the Star Trek episode "Plato's Stepchildren" had Captain Kirk kissing black officer Lt. Uhura, which scandalized those against integration. During the filming of the scene, network executives demanded that two versions be shot—and the one that was used is from Kirk's back so you never see the couple's lips meet.
- In the 1960s, shows like I Dream of Jeannie and Gilligan's Island were required to cover up the belly buttons of women who had two-piece outfits.
- On Norman Lear's All in the Family in the 1970s, they didn't allow a shot of Archie changing his grandson's diaper because it showed the baby's bare bottom.
- On the first season of Happy Days, Fonzie was not allowed to be shown wearing his leather jacket when he was away from his motorcycle—the network thought it would be a bad example to kids since leather jackets were worn then by troublemakers. Producers got creative by bringing the motorcycle into the house or restaurant so he could keep his jacket on! It made no sense to have him leaning on his motorcycle in the living room, but it made it past the censors.

- In the 1980s, Steven Bochco attempted to add more raunchy material to his dramas. So L.A. Law shot a scene of Corbin Bernsen getting out of bed with a bare bottom--but censors cut it.
- In 1991 Seinfeld was not allowed to say "schmuck."
- The Simpsons couldn't have Marge say "get off me" to Homer in bed and instead she had to say "get away from me."
- The Latina maid on Will & Grace was called a "hot tamale" but the line had to be redubbed a day before it aired to call her "hot honey."
- After 9/11 some scripted series digitally removed the World Trade Center towers from the New York City skyline of episodes already shot.
- After the reaction to the Janet Jackson Super Bowl fiasco, networks became stricter, such as blurring the baby's bare bottom on Family Guy, even though four years earlier the same episode aired without censorship.
- American Idol's 2009 runner-up Adam Lambert performed live on the American Music Awards, where he kissed a male dancer and shoved his crotch in the face of another. Over 1500 callers complained to ABC and when the special aired on the west coast the offensive parts had been cut. He was soon dropped from making appearances on Good Morning America and ABC's New Years Eve show, which Lambert claimed was "gay discrimination."
- South Park aired a 2010 episode that included an animated representation of the prophet Muhammad (despite threats that producers would be killed) but at the last minute the image was blocked by a big black box and Comedy Central cut 35 seconds of potentially offensive dialogue.
- MTV promoted a first season episode of Jersey Shore with an explosive shot of Snooki being sucker-punched in the face by a male bar patron, who was arrested. The promotional clip aired on all the entertainment programs and it was one of the most gut-wrenching scenes in reality TV history. But when the actual episode aired the punch was nowhere to be seen because MTV edited the segment after being accused of promoting violence against women and Domino's Pizza pulled its ads.

- MTV also issued a rare public apology in June of 2010 when its censor didn't catch all the f-words uttered at the live telecast of the MTV Movie Awards. The show contained 50 bleeped profanities and yet 12 f-words got through. Although the FCC does not fine for cable profanity, the network cut the words in reruns.
- A Sesame Street preview clip of singer Katy Perry in a low-cut dress chasing Elmo popped up on the Internet and was cut from airing on PBS after parents objected.

The problem is that society's "standards" continue to change. The line for what's appropriate is ever-moving and often makes little sense. Smoking and using guns to kill bad guys, which were staples of 1950s shows, are rarely seen today due to political correctness. Sex jokes and profanity, even in "family" programs, are now okay.

Subjects that never used to be allowed on the tube have entire series written around them. HBO's Big Love makes polygamy acceptable and its series True Blood focuses on vampire sex and murder. Showtime's Dexter is about a sympathetic serial killer. Game of Thrones has included bestiality and incest.

HBO's Hung was about a high school coach who was also a male prostitute. That led to The Hard Times of RJ Berger, an MTV comedy about a high school kid whose life changes when his pants get pulled down and everyone discovers his lengthy body part. Lifetime has done well with The Client List, about a "normal" single mom who gives handjobs at a massage parlor to earn a living.

Cable networks keeps pushing the line and are showered with industry awards for it. The irony is that while totally inappropriate subject matter becomes accepted through long-running series, minor offenses still get cut by networks.

For example, MTV agreed to tone down the Italian stereotypes on Jersey Shore after UNICO, an Italian-American service organization, complained about the term "guido" and misuse of the Italian flag. Of all the things to worry about on Jersey Shore (drinking, sex in the hot tub, violence, profanity) the one thing MTV cuts is the use of the Italian flag?

CBS refused to allow its stars to appear on the prime time Jay Leno Show on rival NBC. CBS entertainment president Nina Tassler said it wasn't a boycott, but it was a competitive move to keep Leno from getting better ratings when a CBS star appeared.

Not only was that illogical, since appearing on a rival network could also raise CBS's ratings, but it's another example of hidden censorship that viewers aren't usually aware of.

The Broadcast Standards departments at networks also watch more than 50,000 ads a year. Less than one percent get cut or rejected since most advertisers want to be careful how their product is portrayed. But censorship still occurs for condoms, guns, sexual stimulants, hard liquor or advocacy groups like PETA. A Website for cheating husbands called AshleyMadison.com has had its ads aired on some male-oriented cable networks but rejected by mainstream broadcasters. The company even tried to put spots in the Super Bowl and the Oscars telecast but was rejected.

One of the most controversial ads that ever aired on Super Bowl Sunday was from a pro-family Christian group that used Florida quarterback Tim Tebow to simply praise his mother. Although there was nothing objectionable about the ad's content, the hidden message of the spot was pro-life (since she had been told by doctors to abort the child that became the football star), which caused liberal groups to demand that it not air.

Broadcasters have also refused to air ads for prescription drugs if the people in the ad are smiling, since the FDA requires that every drug ad have a "fair balance" of risk and rewards. That's why many of the prescription drug ads have a lot of bland straight-faced talking, like a doctor simply sitting at a desk explaining the side effects to a staring patient.

Since 1971 smoking ads on TV have been banned by an act of Congress. Networks have even tried to avoid showing characters smoking. Mad Men was originally supposed to be shown on broadcast television, but programmers said it would have to be done without all the smoking. So producers pitched it to classic movie channel AMC, where smoking is regularly seen in old films.

The Congressional ban on cigarette ads is one of the rare cases of true government censorship. In all of this discussion about viewer freedom and what Americans should be allowed to see, why are there no protests about the government ban of cigarette ads on television? That truly is a First Amendment issue.

The reason is that Americans expect the government to get involved when it comes to health or safety issues. If a fake weight loss product is being advertised, the public expects the government to step in and "censor" the business to avoid false claims. If a bad stock trader is "guaranteeing" 20% interest on an investment, people support the government stepping in and "censoring" false advertising.

So despite all the talk of supporting the First Amendment and freedom of speech, most viewers expect the government to censor groups that lie or deceive in television ads.

We tend to think that one of the places on TV where the First Amendment is operating is during newscasts with people allowed to say whatever they want, right? Wrong. Although news is not usually under FCC rules nor directly edited by Broadcast Standards departments, there is a type of internal news censorship that does occur.

News departments are filled with reporters, editors and news directors that spend the day deciding what to air and what not to air. That is a type of censorship, because these journalists make value-based decisions regarding what is newsworthy. Then within a story they make judgments on what views should be shown and whose opinions get aired.

News judgments are made every minute of every day. If Barack Obama campaigns in Iowa and there is a group of protestors holding up signs, a newscast decides whether to show the protestors. If the reporter fails to show them is the story really balanced? Does it make a difference if there are 20 or 200 in the anti-Obama crowd? What if they were all war veterans and it's Memorial Day weekend?

Those are decisions news reporters and producers have to make. Then turn around and ask what the station would do if Obama's opponent in the last election, Mitt Romney, had the same protestors show up.

If Obama had a crowd of 1000 inside but 20 protestors from a a local "peace" group outside, they would probably be ignored. For Romney the protestors would not only be shown but one of them would be interviewed blaming Republicans for the bloodshed in the world and it would look like the city was against the candidate. Reporters and producers skew the story based on their political biases and pre-conceived notions of what makes a good story.

Broadcast journalists make decisions every day that impact how you view a story that is being reported and it is a form of censorship. When they repeatedly only give you one lop-sided view of a politician or criminal or entertainer then they are making choices that amount to censorship.

Bill Clinton is shown as a wise elderly statesman. Lindsay Lohan is a party girl in need of rehab. Trayvon Martin was just buying some candy at a convenience store and innocently walking home while George Zimmerman was a trigger-happy racist neighborhood watchman who killed the boy. All are distorted, one-sided pictures of complicated people, created by reporters who leave out key details that amount to censorship.

This is a sensitive issue to me because I have personally been interviewed for a number of national TV news stories, and know that reporters have agendas that don't let facts get in the way. When I was interviewed for the CBS Evening News, the correspondent spent 90 minutes with me and had plenty of footage to choose from. When the report aired, he used two short clips that completely misrepresented my opinion on the subject of television preachers (which I have been an expert on since 1981).

So when he asked if I thought all TV ministers were crooks, I responded with something like, "Some people say all TV preachers are crooks and con men. But I don't believe that because some of the ministries do good." The report then aired with the reporter saying a professor was warning people not to trust the ministers because (cut to a shot of me saying) "all TV preachers are crooks and con men."

Did I say that? Well…yes, but by cutting out the first and last words of what I originally said, the reporter actually had me saying the opposite of what I believed. And that was the CBS Evening News, supposedly one of the great news organizations in broadcasting. He took my words out of context and edited my quote to fit his version of the story—which is a form of censorship.

This is the same CBS News that showed anchorman Dan Rather sitting in front of New York City's Times Square. In the background there was an ad for NBC on a giant screen that overseas the famous crossroads. CBS electronically blurred the NBC ad, not wanting to promote a competitor. That is not only censorship but also a breech of journalistic ethics to change the picture you are shooting.

Another example that I witnessed involves the 2000 presidential election, where the Supreme Court decided George Bush won the disputed count even though Al Gore received more actual votes. The controversy involved "hanging chad" votes cast in Florida. Reporters swarmed a Miami building where recounts occurred and each of the major networks covered what they called a "city in protest" from the sidewalk in front of the courthouse.

Video showed the faces of loud, violent protesters objecting to the Bush victory. Each newscast told of the uproar in the city, noting that blacks and Hispanics felt their votes hadn't counted.

But one TV news camera operator decided to zoom out from across the street and show the truth of what was happening. It revealed that only 8 or 10 protestors were actually in front of the building—surrounded by a couple dozen media members getting the story! Meanwhile average citizens were going about their business as they walked past on the sidewalk. This was not an outraged city preparing to riot—this was a few people getting face time on camera and the media shooting only close-up shots that misled viewers into thinking the situation was much worse than it was.

That type of distorted coverage is a form of censorship, to the point that it could be called propaganda. TV news reporters and producers are misleading the public in order to make a much more interesting and dramatic story that often supports the reporter's political beliefs. The fact that all three networks chose to handle the Bush voting story the same way shows an industry-wide bias in how the story was approached, treating it as an entire city upset that the Republican won.

If you have any doubts about biased media, simply do a study of how television news treats President Barack Obama verses how they reported on George Bush's presidency. The Pew Center conducted research that showed in the first six months in office, each administration introduced support of similar faith-based programs to help those in need. When Bush came up with the concept in 2001, there was dramatic media criticism of the plan to have a person in the White House who would help coordinate religious groups feeding the hungry and housing the homeless. The media objected on the grounds of separation of church and state.

When Obama did the exact same thing eight years later as one of his first acts in office, even proposing to elevate the religious program to an official advisory council, the media praised the new president for his compassionate approach to helping the needy without using tax dollars.

Studies also show Obama mentioned his faith and invoked the name Jesus more often than Bush did, with no concerns stated from the same press that so violently feared Bush was imposing his religious views on the country.

Another example is how the media treated the two presidents' love of playing golf. Bush was slammed when he took to the links while soldiers were fighting in Iraq, called "a callow, lazy, rich boy." So in 2003 Bush stopped all golf while in office after playing 24 rounds in his first 33 months.

Obama played 41 rounds of golf in just his first 18 months in office while conducting wars in Iraq and Afghanistan. He even played two rounds the weekend after the oil crisis in the Gulf of Mexico and continued to play while thousands were suffering on the shores, hitting the course eight of the nine weekends after the "worst environmental disaster in U.S. history."

Obama played twice as much golf as Bush in his first years in office. Yet when Republicans raised questions as to why Obama wasn't being held to the same standard, the media defended Obama saying that he needed the sport to relieve the pressure of the presidency!

Bush was criticized almost immediately for his mishandling of Hurricane Katrina after it took four days for him to sign a relief package. Yet it took five weeks for the press to point out the Obama's lack of leadership in the Gulf oil crisis, and that was only after a heated condemnation by former Clinton advisor James Carville, who went on TV and told President Obama, "Man, you have got to get down here and take control of this! Put somebody in charge of this and get this thing moving! We're about to die down here."

Broadcasting magazine was one of the few to put it in perspective, saying the Obama administration had "hesitancy to take ownership of the plague" and noted that the media failed to take Obama to task. That's because the press don't treat a crisis during the Obama administration as being one he caused but instead one that was an unfortunate distraction thrust on him. Analyst Andrew Tyndall said, "The political angle they're running with at the moment is not that Obama's being incompetent, but that he isn't projecting the right image."

Distorting or spinning news comes from both liberal and conservative reporters and cable commentators. Fox News gets big ratings for doing it toward the right but MSNBC and CNN do the same thing toward the left. Whenever they intentionally fail to report all the facts, it is a form of censorship. The same is true if they mislead by failing to put it in the proper context. Some of what you see that is called news is actually a distorted, subjective account that skews information, filtered through the TV personality's own political beliefs.

One famous example was when The CBS Evening News reported on a story about an aborted fetus found in a trash bin. It put an electronic blob over a picture of the body, saying it was too graphic for viewers to see. Anti-abortion groups had a legitimate question—if it is legally considered merely tissue and not a child, then why not show it? Pro-abortion groups claim that if the fetus is shown then people might conclude it really is a human life that should not be aborted, so they are anti-choice when it comes to letting viewers see the aborted fetus! CBS sided with the pro-abortion groups and censored the image.

That is similar to a story covered by a leading TV news station in Des Moines involving a truck driving through town with a giant anti-abortion image of an aborted fetus on the side. Viewers saw video of the truck, but the photo of the fetus was electronically blurred.

The same local news outlet during the H1N1 "bird flu" crisis in 2009, where citizens lined up to get shots of the vaccine, blurred the images of needles being put into people's arms fearing that it would offend news viewers! No matter how well intentioned, it is a form of censorship and unethical journalism.

In 2010, that same leading local station said they would refuse to air video of a Florida pastor who was planning on burning copies of the Koran on the ninth anniversary of 9/11. Even though this was a major worldwide news story with potential political ramifications, the Associated Press, Fox News and other major media outlets also said they wouldn't show any footage of the burning.

Not only is that censorship, but it is inconsistent with the coverage by those same organizations of Bible burning, flag burning and George Bush effigy burning. The irony is that even though TV newscasts decided to censor the pastor's Koran burning before it even happened, those same stations had no problem that very week showing protesting Muslims burning an effigy of the pastor!

Some condemned the media for giving any coverage to the preacher, saying such opinions should not be shown. Television commentators remarked, "We shouldn't tolerate intolerance." Newscasters often make such statements when it comes to conservatives speaking out about any subject that is near and dear to journalists (gay marriage, marijuana legalization, Democrats caught in a scandal, etc.).

Think about it…to not tolerate intolerance is to do the very thing that is being condemned and is hypocritical. It actually promotes censorship. So the same press that screams First Amendment freedom of speech does not support the free speech rights of those they disagree with.

When the news program 20/20 was ready to air an expose of Senator Ted Kennedy in the 1980s, it was pulled two days before it went on the air. The reason? The head of ABC News Roone Arledge was pals with the Kennedy family and didn't want the nasty truths about the senator revealed. It wasn't that the piece was wrong or even unfair—it was simply that the ABC News President used his power to censor what the public saw. Who knows if airing that piece would have changed history.

It was no surprise when television coverage of Kennedy's death in 2009 treated him like he was a saint. For decades the press knew the true stories about his vices (which even the senator admitted to in his autobiography released after his death), but reporters chose to censor what they told the American people, creating a false image of the man. After his funeral many broadcast journalists admitted that they glossed over his failings to not detract from his political agenda, which they supported.

These stories are just a few examples that point to the conclusion that "censorship" is something every network and station does daily by making choices regarding what they show you. Those decisions are made for economic, creative or political reasons, and the viewing public is free to protest the content choices. But in the end the networks can pretty much do what they want and you have few "rights" other than to turn the channel.

Chapter Five Discussion Questions

1. How do networks censor in their everyday decisions?
2. How does broadcasting not necessarily meet the definition of free speech covered by the First Amendment?
3. What are a couple of examples of absurd TV censorship?
4. How have standards changed over the years? What subjects are allowed on the air today? Yet what small things still get complained about?
5. How do ads get censored? What about smoking ads?
6. How does TV news censor? What did the author personally learn?
7. Explain how censorship can also be what choices are made in how something is presented on TV? How has the coverage of Obama vs. Bush been an example?

Chapter Six

CHILDREN & FAMILY VIEWING

Most college students are part of a generation that has been raised from birth with the television on. They think nothing of sitting in front of the tube all day, wasting time because there's "nothing else to do." These young adults were raised with constant noise and visual stimulation, and think it odd to hear a professor suggest that television may have had any kind of negative impact on them.

After almost three decades of requiring students to control their media habits for a three-day TV diet that I assign in my course, I have concluded that 85 to 90% of all young people are addicted to electronic visual stimulation. Even they admit it after completing the assignment. They can't comprehend living a life without something to constantly keep them entertained.

Those students grow up to become working adults, parents and contributing members of society. Yet their need for visual stimulation doesn't decline with time. If anything it gets worse. As stress fills their adult lives, they turn to the tube for comfort. It allows them to escape the pressures of the everyday world and distracts their minds so they don't have to "think."

If that describes you, then you are typical. You may say to yourself that TV doesn't mean that much to you, and you would be just like every other adult I have encountered who thinks television has little impact on them. But trust me, almost everyone would go crazy if they were required to go without it while not being able to replace it with other electronic devices. They, like most of my students, are media addicts. And so possibly are you.

You like noise because it keeps you from thinking and covers up the problems in life. You are usually bored by anything "old fashioned" like reading books, playing board games, having intellectual conversations or just "wasting time" doing nothing.

As a matter of fact, you probably try to avoid silence at all costs. You constantly use iPods, cell phones, computers and TV sets—proudly juggling two or three of them at the same time! You share your need for noise with the media-addicted people around you, like roommates, friends and family members.

You get help in feeding your addiction from places you visit like sports bars and coffee shops. You like to have music on while you work. You shop while talking on a cell phone. You exercise at the health club while watching TV. You walk across campus with an ear plug in your ear. You text while talking with someone over dinner. You even keep the TV on to put you to sleep, which means that you live just about every waking hour with electronic stimulation.

Studies show that even with all the other electronic devices available, the TV is the thing you spend the most time with. Television today is virtually everywhere—in cars (with satellite cable channels!), in bathrooms (built into the shower!), at the gas pump (reminding you to get hot dogs inside!), on airplanes (now with dozens of cable channels!), in grocery stores (forecasting a storm today, so pick up some toilet paper!) and, of course, available 24 hours a day on cell phones (the latest one-inch-wide clip on YouTube is hilarious!).

This makes television more pervasive in your life than just about anything other than air and food. Because you have grown up with TV, it surrounds you to the point that you don't even think about it until you freak out when it's gone during a power outage or when you're at a wedding scheduled at the same time as the big game (thank goodness for tiny ear buds so you can secretly listen to the game during the ceremony!).

Life without television would be like trying to breathe at high altitude or scrounging for food while lost in the forest. You feel like you must have TV in order to survive.

The irony is that television programming is only about 65 years old. So there are many people in this country that grew up without it. My parents didn't see TV until they were 17 years old.

Some of your grandparents and great-grandparents can tell you stories of what their childhoods were like before TV. And you can't fathom how anyone could have lived that way. What did they do with their time?

Pretty much everyone since the mid-1950s has had a television set, so it is a given. Oh, your parents or grandparents may tell you a few stories of how they only had a couple channels or how they had rules to get their homework done first. But that seems like ancient history to you, because you were raised with cable TV in your bedroom, instant access to DVDs and video available on your computer.

Media-addicted adults who got enthralled with the new medium in the 50s and 60s passed along their bad habits to their children and grandchildren. Well-meaning parents justify using the TV to keep the kids constantly entertained by thinking it makes the young ones "happy" and even that it helps "educate" them to current events.

But the truth is adults raised you with the TV on so that you wouldn't whine and they would have a cheap babysitter. They let you have a set in your room by the time you were ten, told you to only watch good shows and then shut the door while you were allowed to become emotionally attached to the appliance. Television, to your parents, was always seen as a positive because it made you feel good and allowed them to avoid their parental responsibility while you stared at the tube.

Then, once a week, hardworking helicopter parents (emotionally distant but always trying to hover over the kids activities) would assuage their guilt about rarely seeing their children by spending "quality time" in a "movie night"—with everyone staring at the television set while eating pizza or popcorn.

Wow—isn't TV great? It has become the glue that holds the family together in modern America!

Television even was used as part of the discipline process. If you were bad you were threatened to have your TV time taken away. If you were good you might finally get that flat screen TV you always.

When my daughter was in 4th grade, I waited in the school parking lot on the last day of classes for her to come out with her final report card. As I sat there I saw a little third grader running and screaming toward the car next to me, yelling, "Mom—I get it! I get the color TV for my bedroom! Look, Mom, I got all C's!"

This parent had used the reward of a new TV for her daughter getting all C's on her report card! Was the mother crazy? If the kid was getting D's and F's before then the parent should have kept the child away from the television, not rewarded the kid with a new one in her bedroom for getting C's!

What that type of upbringing means is that children accept television as a positive. It's an expectation that if they are good enough they'll be rewarded with their own TV. It's a right of passage that communicates the start of "growing up."

According to one source, by the time a child is 17, he or she has watched 18,000 hours of television, compared to 11,000 hours in school and 3,000 hours reading. Before they are adults, children see 17,000 murders, 250,000 sex scenes and 350,000 commercials, including 20,000 for war toys and 35,000 for beer and wine.

Other research reveals:

Preschool Children

- Watch 7 hours of TV a day vs. spending 10 minutes a day in quality time with parents.
- By age five, children have already watched over 5,000 hours of television.
- 40% of babies now watch regularly by 3 months. Early viewing "rewires brain" for less ability to concentrate in early elementary school.
- 40% of kids under 5 have TVs in their bedrooms.
- 85% of parents do not monitor what kids ages 3-8 watch.
- So many ads are seen that by age 2 kids have developed brand loyalty.
- 82% of sponsors' messages on PBS are for fast food & junk food.
- Preschoolers who watch 4 hours/day are 30% more likely to be bullies.
- Pediatricians say "too much TV watching by kids…leads to lifelong sub-optimal development"; they recommend a ban on TVs and computers from bedrooms.
- Every hour a day a kid under 3 watches TV doubles the risk of ADHD problems.
- Studies suggest a possible link between infant TV and autism.

Grade School Children

- Watch 4 ½ hours of TV/DVD a day vs. 10 minutes a day spent reading.
- 95% of TV watching by kids over 7 is done alone and unsupervised.
- 2/3's of those 8 and older have TV sets in their bedrooms.
- Kids with TVs in bedrooms scored lowest on standardized tests.
- 3/4 watch TV right before bedtime, which researchers say leads to sleep disorders and kids refusing to go to bed.
- For students aged 9 to 15, any weekday TV viewing results in lower test scores and the more watched on weekdays the lower the scores. Boys are more impacted than girls and children that are allowed to watch R-rated cable movies have the lowest test scores while being the most aggressive at school.
- The amount of weekend viewing has no impact on test scores.
- Doctors say the #1 reason for childhood obesity is watching TV.
- 72% of ads on shows for kids ages 8-12 are for junk food, fast food or candy.

Teenagers

- Watch 4 hours of TV/DVD a day.
- Boys #1 show is Family Guy, Girls #1 show is Gray's Anatomy.
- Pediatrician study shows 2/3 of what teens watch has explicit sex.
- Teens that watch the most TV shows with sexual content are twice as likely to start having sex within a year of seeing the show (not just explicit shows, but even shows that just talk about sex, like sitcoms).
- Kids watching over two hours/day of TV are more likely to become smokers or have high cholesterol as adults.

Adults

- Watch over 5 hours of TV a day; the TV is on for over 8 hours a day in the average home.
- Recent studies suggest a TV viewing/Alzheimer's connection.

- 74% of families watch TV while eating (but only 41% of parents say reading while eating is acceptable).
- Less than 10% of adults that are parents of school children watch TV with their kids.
- A Stanford researcher says, "The media are children's most powerful influence, with the <u>possible</u> exception of parents."

Repeated studies conclude that **watching more than an hour of television a day has a negative impact on children**. TV-addicted youngsters have lower grades, read less, are more aggressively violent and have more problems as adults. There is even some evidence that large amounts of childhood television viewing may give root to long-term mental health issues, including ADHD, OCD and Alzheimer's.

Medical and sociological experts have warned about children watching too much TV. Since 1990, the American Academy of Pediatrics have been issuing almost annual reports that warn parents of the dangers of too much time in front of the tube, encouraging them to limit children's viewing.

For the first few years that the reports were issued, the doctors said viewing should be limited to one hour a day—but when parents refused to listen and complained that it wasn't realistic, the doctors revised the recommendation to two hours a day even though the research shows that **anything beyond an hour a day will negatively impact children**. Today only 11% of the parents say they are putting a viewing limit on children of two hours or less a day.

Research studies have found that:

- Too much TV makes children "stimulus addicts" and keeps them from doing the physical activities that will improve their bodies and brains.
- TV viewing correlates to obesity and diabetes both in children and adults. Those that watch over two hours a day as kids have triple the rate of childhood obesity and diabetes, while obesity in adults was highest for people who had television sets in the bedroom as children.
- There is a "displacement factor" where kids watch television at the expense of brain-using activities like playing or reading. They also play video games or rock band instead of participating in sports or playing a real instrument. TV takes the place of creative and physical activities that expand mental capabilities.
- "TV induces a vegetative state" according to one study (that was later duplicated), which concludes that watching television lowers a child's metabolic rate. These studies said that children burn more calories sleeping or sitting doing nothing than they do when watching television because a person's metabolism rate is lowest when watching the tube!
- Television "numbs children physically" and work as a type of painkiller when soothing a child.
- Young children imitate the negatives that they see on television even if they are told its wrong or it's seen in the context of teaching children something positive.
- An Iowa State University long-term study found that playing video games leads to shortened attention spans. Those who play video games for more than two hours a day have decreased attention at school and the effect continues into college. The researchers concluded video games have the same negative effect on college students as they have on elementary students. The more time spent playing video games, the less the student is able to focus on schoolwork.

When kids have mental or physical disorders, the last thing parents want to do is blame TV. In trying to help calm the child, parents actually increase the use of TV—seemingly unaware that they are contributing to the very disabilities they are trying to solve.

Studies have shown the same is true for children with sleep disorders. Instead of turning the TV off when a child has trouble sleeping, parents let the child fall asleep with the television on thinking it will help the insomnia. Instead they are actually adding to the problem.

Educational experts also see the negative impact of TV on children:

- Studies shows that TV can help a child educationally...but only if the child is limited to one hour a day of television and the programs watched are mentally stimulating, not just entertainment-driven.
- "Educational" videos for babies have actually been found to "impede language development." Children that had watched the most videos when under the age of two actually knew fewer words than other children on a language test when they got older. Doctors warn to not let children under age two watch any TV!
- Specialized shows like Sesame Street do not increase language skills in the long run and ultimately turn children into passive learners. The show has been called "counterproductive" for most children, is said to induce aggressive behavior, disconnects children from human family members, has commercialized stereotyped characters and is "the ultimate short attention span theatre."

Obviously Sesame Street and other children's "educational" programming teach some good things. But Neil Postman, author of "Amusing Ourselves to Death," wrote:

> "Parents embraced Sesame Street for several reasons, among them that it assuaged their guilt over the fact they could not or would not restrict their children's access to television. Sesame Street appeared to justify allowing a four or five year old to sit transfixed in front of a TV screen for unnatural periods of time...Sesame Street relieved them of the responsibility of teaching their pre-school children how to read...in a culture where children are apt to be considered a nuisance...."

"We know that Sesame Street encourages children to love school, (but) only if school is like Sesame Street. Which is to say we now know that Sesame Street undermines what the traditional idea of schooling represents."

For 12 years I volunteered with my children's' schools and discovered a shockingly large amount of teachers using entertainment television in the classroom. It includes:

- The third grade "teacher of the year" for the district showing a full-length Disney animated movie once or twice a week. When I asked her about it she said she needs the time to grade papers.
- A 7th grade teacher had students watch Toy Story in math, justifying it by saying that math was involved in the computer work to create the animation.
- An 8th grade history class watched the Disney cartoon Pocahontas, with the teacher saying it was a lesson in Native American history.
- The 9th grade Spanish class watched the comedy film Three Amigos to help with translation.
- Even 10th grade PE showed a movie--National Lampoon's Christmas Vacation, saying it was a way to show students how to "reduce stress."
- "Channel One" is a school news service that provides video monitors to schools in exchange for the commitment that all students are required to watch the daily news program (that includes commercials aimed at the kids). One student who was reading was sent to detention for not watching the TV because the school can lose the equipment if the viewing is not enforced.

Another study concluded that parents and teachers ignore the research that shows the negative impact of the media on young people. It said adults are "deluded" regarding the impact of television—they say they use it as a learning device and don't think they're using it as a babysitter. Parents dismiss studies showing television hurts a child's intellectual development.

The reason adults are in denial is that most are unwilling to limit their own viewing time so they don't want to be "hypocrites" by limiting their children's time or taking the TV set out of the bedroom. Studies show that even though parents think society is losing its moral base, they don't believe the warnings about the impact of television applies to their own kids—only to others' kids.

The government has attempted to get involved over the years by putting rules on children's television programming. The most sweeping change started in 1996, when the Clinton White House held a summit that resulted in placing major requirements on broadcast stations as part of the "Children's Television Act."

Broadcast stations (not cable networks) now must air three hours of educational programs each week that are clearly identified with either a description or symbol showing that it's educational. The shows can meet either intellectual or social educational needs. Qualifying programs must air between 7 a.m. and 10 p.m. and must be reported as part of an annual FCC report.

After the rules were implemented, there was actually a decline in the amount of intellectual programs for children, replaced by series that emphasized only social skills. Instead of teaching math, science or language, children's programs started emphasizing concepts like treating others with respect. And the new rules resulted in an increase in cartoon violence, since resolving conflict can be an educational social message that meets the FCC's rules.

There's also a new "two click" rule regarding what Websites can be advertised to children. A site mentioned in a TV ad during a children's program must be educational, forcing advertisers to set up informative Web pages that won't promote a product until the second click.

The FCC even launched its own site to deal with children's issues at www.FCC.gov/kidszone. It also has a new site for parents at http://reboot.FCC.gov/parents.

The government agency has also proposed "a la carte" (pay per channel) cable programming, so that cable systems be required to sell customers only the channels they want. The FCC feels that would help keep children from watching inappropriate programs and would encourage parents to only subscribe to family-friendly networks. Some cable systems have already started to offer family packages but few people are subscribing because it keeps adults from watching networks they like. If true pay-per-channel cable were to be forced through for everyone, the cost per network would probably quadruple and make it more expensive to subscribe to cable or satellite while receiving fewer channels.

The reality is that government intervention won't work because most parents don't want to change their own habits to create a healthier viewing environment for their children. Just like parents set a bad example in front of children by eating junk food, drinking alcohol and smoking, modern adults think nothing of allowing a 5 year old to watch adult cable and pay channels like HBO. Young children are allowed to watch a violent PG-13 movie ("he's very mature for his age," parents will claim) and in some cases even allow small children to watch R-rated content ("she doesn't really understand the adult parts—it's way over her head").

Children's television activist Peggy Charren said, "Parents don't like to think of themselves as bad parents." Adults don't want to say "no" to kids and don't want to appear "mean" or "hypocritical," so they let kids watch what they want and then say they're being good parents.

Pediatric Professor Vic Strasburger of University of New Mexico said, "Unfortunately, parents tend to be relatively clueless. They're too busy with their own jobs and lives, and they think their kids are safe if they're in the den watching TV."

Today when networks put on what they call a "family" show, it is usually the non-traditional family with very adult situations, like Two and a Half Men. How I Met Your Mother uses the offensive gimmick that children are being told the very adult sexual story of how their parents hooked up. Even Glee has been called a family show, although some began to question the series after a lesbian kiss popped up between teen cheerleaders and cast members posed provocatively in adult magazines.

If you are looking for family comedies on a network with "family" in the title, you're looking in the wrong place. ABC Family may be the most deceptively-titled network on cable, calling itself "A New Kind of Family." The Disney-owned channel seems to go out of its way to be edgy and offend with series about drunken frat parties, skanky cheerleaders and a pregnant unwed 15-year-old (with the network warning: viewer discretion advised!).

Melissa and Joey is an ABC Family sitcom featuring former child stars Melissa Joan Hart (Sabrina the Teenage Witch) and Joey Lawrence (Blossom). The show is about a party girl-turned-politician who loves to drink and partners with a bankrupt financial advisor to take care of the kids of her jailed sister. Its first episode featured talk about strippers, drinking at age 15, profanities and a recurring joke about a teen girl's poem that mentions a female body part that rhymes with "Lunt."

Even though it airs in the old family viewing hour of 7 p.m. on a channel with "Family" in the title, the stars told *Entertainment Weekly* that the series is not for kids. Lawrence said, "ABC Family's really pushing the limits. It's not anywhere near the Disney Channel. We're talking about vaginas." Hart added, "We don't cross the line, we're not HBO. But don't let your 8-year-old watch."

The "adultification" of family comedies is even starting to be used by the Disney Channel and Nickelodeon. Middle-aged adult men create "kid" shows that contain crude humor and sexual innuendo. Good Luck Charlie was created by the former producer of Cheers, the bar-based adult hit. The Fred Show is produced by the same guy who did One Tree Hill.

A Nickelodeon series called The Naked Brothers Band had little boys acting like stoned '60s rockers (creators claimed it was a kids version of Spinal Tap) and it was written/directed by the boys' real-life mother, a former actress from the very adult show Thirtysomething. Not only did many parents find the show's title offensive, but an image in the pilot episode showed the youngsters getting drunk on soda pop and doing kiddy versions of having a hangover.

These programs are merely children speaking words from the minds of very adult writers and producers. Dan Schneider, the 47-year-old creator of iCarly, Victorious, Drake & Josh and Zoey 101, says he considers himself childlike, but the fact that he is unmarried and has no children himself makes one wonder how he is able to write for them.

Misguided adults that think there's nothing wrong with a child watching Disney or Nickelodeon never seriously look at the issue of how television will impact children. They fear their children will "miss out" if they don't watch what everyone else in their peer group watches. Parents don't want the child to be a social outcast or "weird," so they accept any TV viewing as helping the child assimilate to society.

Some adults fight their own strict upbringing by raising children with "no censorship" that would limit a child's ability to learn, so they just let the kid watch anything he wants. Those parents then spend years trying to figure out why the child has become distant or aggressive or anxious or psychotic.

TV Guide writer Susan Stewart allows her elementary-aged daughters to watch Law & Order. The writer bragged, "We live in a TV world. TV are us. I see my responsibility as a parent as not to stand between my children and the television set, but to sit next to them on the couch while we watch TV." While the idea of watching with her children is good, why isn't she choosing age-appropriate content to view and discuss together? The answer is because Stewart herself wants to watch Law & Order and in order to spend time with her kids she plants them next to her on the couch!

Another mom watches CSI with her toddler and doesn't think the gory scenes are a problem. She says, "They're reality." Even worse, over one-third of parents surveyed allow ten year olds to watch pay cable R-rated movies.

The problem with television and children isn't the TV and isn't the children—it is bad parenting. Adults don't want to have to work at being parents. They don't want to induce conflict by saying "no." So they give the child over to the tube and justify it by claiming it's "educational." Then the adults go in another room and satisfy their own television addictions. It is dysfunctional parenting, passing bad habits from one generation to the next.

The solution is not to throw out the TV or to lock up the kids. It's to have adults take control of the television in the household and teach children similar self-control in utilizing the medium. That includes creating very specific household guidelines, such as:

- Only having one TV in the home, with no sets in bedrooms. (I can hear readers raised in homes with eight TVs saying, "Is he crazy?" No, it is actually possible to have only one television in a home!)
- Putting the TV in a room far away from the main living area, then sticking it in an entertainment center with doors that close so you can't see the TV when you come into the room.
- Scheduling and limiting viewing time. Turn viewing into an event, like going to the movie theater.
- Watching only recorded programs in order to not waste time on commercials or inappropriate shows.
- Watching with the children so you can discuss what they have just seen and have more shared family time.
- Subscribe to cable networks and pay for a digital video recorder--but only if you are able to use them to control your viewing. Cable gives you many more educational and moral options than broadcast television. When you don't have cable or don't record programs, you tend to

watch a lot of broadcast network junk that you normally wouldn't waste time on.
- Get rid of cable and only watch on the computer—but only if you can control the millions of online options (which is very difficult).

These guidelines may seem like a return to the dark ages for some people. But it leads to you being in control of the television instead of the television being in control of you.

If you have any doubts about whether you should try to control your habits, read the words of my students who struggled to go three days on my TV diet. Many of them use words like "need" and "addicted" to describe television as a necessity.

Scott said, "I always have to watch...I realize that I need TV in my life." Josh wrote, "I found that I need what little time I do get to lay around watching TV...I also need time to space out and let media do the thinking for me." Breanne commented that at 2 a.m., "I needed my friend, my TV."

Andy said, "I realize now that TV is a drug. It's addictive and it is hard to control." Brian said, "There was a point during the week that I felt I was going crazy without TV."

Another student named Andy wrote, "I'm addicted. I'm a junkie hooked on live satellite feeds and the top ten shows. I'd like to say that TV doesn't rule my life with an iron first, but that would be an outright lie. TV consumes me. It eats me alive and digests me within its belly. I think I need help."

Autumn wrote, "It's clear to me that people in today's society have been trained to make many forms of entertainment involuntary action. Our ears and eyes have been taught to need television and radio rather than want it." She also defiantly didn't follow the assignment completely because "I felt I was torturing myself." So she concluded, "I am capable of breaking my addiction if I need to but I won't give it up until I see it as 100% negative."

Pam said, "To go through a week without watching television is like going to the dentist—painful." Angie said, "I do acknowledge that I use TV to numb my brain."

Another wrote, "Giving birth might be easier than giving up my TV." While Chris said that during his time on the diet, "I found myself pacing around sometimes in front of the set like an expectant father. I also found out that I don't watch TV so much for the content as I just have it on because I crave the company it can provide."

One started her paper with, "My name is Laura and I am a TV addict...I'm letting a little box with knobs control me...I hate being controlled, particularly by an inanimate object."

Alex wrote, "I am addicted to television...All the stresses, all the homework and all of my busy life was consumed by a 19-inch brain-sucking device...I have learned that I am truly abandoning the relationships with the people I love the most by watching television."

Harlan summarized what everyone was thinking when he wrote, "I couldn't imagine a world without TV being a world that I'd want to live in...I couldn't live happily without TV. I could live, but it would just make me feel like I was missing something."

Tim, whose parents had put restrictions on his TV viewing when he was a child, said, "Now that I am an adult, I watch TV every chance I get. I am addicted and probably always will be."

Samantha wrote, "I am sick of school, my job and Des Moines...The only thing that I can do that I love is to watch TV...I watch it so I don't have to think and so I can relax."

John said, "I use television as a way to escape my boredom." But he learned, "It is almost scary the hold, impact and influence it has on our lives."

Chris admitted, "TV screws up my ability to think critically."

Barb wrote that she was in a fairly serious relationship until the television was turned off. The TV was used by the couple to avoid arguments and once it went off the conflict began. She also said she uses the television to get over anxiety issues associated with an experience with a stalker. She has to fall asleep with the TV on or she feels scared. Without television, she wrote, "I would just lay there and think of bad possible things that could happen."

Terra struggled with her boyfriend, using the TV to avoid decisions and conflict, saying, "Television was the third person in our relationship." She concluded, "I found that while TV may not cause me to get lung cancer, it does have a great effect on my life."

Many substituted other things for television when they were asked to not watch. Some admitted that they got drunk, a number of them went on shopping sprees, a few gambled away hundreds of dollar, three started smoking, a couple of them admitted doing drugs, and others mentioned having more sex (including a guy who paid for it and a girl who picked up a stranger at a bar for a one night stand).

But there were positive outcomes as well. A number of students felt their relationships improved when they had more time to just talk or play board games or exercise. The boyfriend of Jessica saw she was frustrated not being able to watch TV and right there on the couch "he gave me my engagement ring...It was a terrific night and TV never entered my mind." She wrote in her paper, "There is more to life than TV and TV is not reality."

Giovanna said, "TV is an escape for me. It is an escape from everything." She falls asleep with the television on, but when she was forced to turn the tube off, "I found myself starting to have a better relationship with my family...I was more active and got more things done. I started to wonder what the world would have been like without TV."

Lindsay said turning the TV off allowed her to spend "quality time" with her live-in boyfriend. "At first it was difficult for my relationship but by the end of the week we found ourselves rekindling our romance and relationship. In the past when we used to fight we both used the TV for distraction...but now we are verbally expressing our emotions and it makes it easier for us to know how each other is feeling."

Josh wrote: "I have continued to limit my television use. This has made both my girlfriend and I happier because our relationship has grown closer together throughout the diet and after. I have also become a healthier person due to the television diet. Most importantly, I feel that I am a more driven person because instead of spending my time watching TV, I instead spend my time finding ways I can better my future."

Heather said she and her boyfriend went camping when she had to go without television and "had an absolute blast...it was the most fun I'd had in years...This class has been a life saver not only to me, but for my future children. I have decided that I do not want a television in the house."

Brandon started reading books, exercising and cutting back on junk food. He concluded, "The quality of my activities was much higher without TV and my attention span increased as well...TV can have such a huge impact on a person's life, whether they realize it or not. I think many people are not willing to accept the impact that TV has on them."

Not all endings were happy. This exercise caused many young adults to face their bitter emotions about how television impacted their families.

Nancy wrote that her mother had been diagnosed with bipolar disorder, depression and multiple personality disorder. "My mom would do two things: sit and watch TV, or go and spend money." She said that her mother refuses to turn off the television and Nancy "couldn't wait for the day to be able to move out on my own...I do not want to end up like my mom...I have completely lost my mother to TV."

Tom was raised by a dad who ignored the kids in order to watch television. Tom wrote, "I am an angry young man at the age of 25. I go to my parents' house and it never fails that my dad is sprawled out on the couch watching TV...Once a person realizes my intense bitterness, it is not difficult to understand why I have no desire to even have a television in my house. I think it is a waste of time. I think it consumes the minutes and steals the years. I don't want lost years."

Laurie had a family that always ate meals with the television on, so during the TV diet she asked them to turn it off. Her dad responded that if she couldn't watch TV, then she'd have to go eat in her room. She wrote, "That's when I realized that my dad loved TV more than he loved me."

When Beth asked her parents to turn the TV sound down so she wouldn't hear it, they ignored her. It reminded her of her childhood. "There were times it hurt to see them choose TV over me, but what hurt the most was when I'd want to share something I did in school or get help with some homework and they'd say, 'Shhh, I want to see this show.' It was those times, not this diet, that taught me how TV invades and takes over people's lives. It made me take control of my life because I will never put television before my children."

Chapter Six Discussion Questions

1. How does the typical person use the tube? How is television today literally everywhere? How have parents contributed to the problem?
2. How many hours do children spend watching TV compared to school and reading? What type of ads do they see?
3. Select a couple of the research results listed about children that surprise you.
4. What do the pediatricians recommend and why did they change the original recommendation?
5. What have medical and educational studies found out about children's TV viewing?
6. What's wrong with Sesame Street?
7. There are examples of teachers using TV at school in an odd way. Did you ever experience this?
8. How did the Children's Television Act add rules?
9. What do people say about blaming adults for the problem?
10. What are reasons parents allow their children to watch unlimited TV?
11. What's so bad about ABC Family, Disney Channel or Nickelodeon?
12. What are solutions for taking control of the television?
13. What responses from student papers surprise you? Can you relate to anything they say?

Chapter Seven

TELEVISION'S GREATEST PROGRAMS

Attempts have often been made to list the greatest television shows of all time. Some take a sweeping view of the medium, while others focus on a specific genre. None ever seem to use any type of measuring stick and instead depend upon the whims of the current writers of pop culture to decide which programs make the list.

Online lists of the greatest TV programs are too bound to the recent past and give less importance to older series. Instead of looking back over the entire 65 years of TV programming, modern writers focus on the fad shows that are popular now.

For example, when Lost ended in 2010, many of the articles about the finale talked about how it was one of the greatest shows in history. But only four percent of the population regularly watched the last season of the program with viewership dropping over the years due to confusing plotlines. It's possible that twenty years from now few will even recall the series.

You don't believe it? Then look at what were considered "great" TV shows twenty years ago. Murphy Brown is a name recognized by some middle-aged people but young people don't know what it was. Designing Women, L.A. Law and Evening Shade were considered cutting-edge hits back then, but no one today is talking about them.

Since I have taught students for almost 30 years, I have gone through the shifts in popular culture. For every Cosby Show, which pretty much everyone still knows about a generation later, there is a Hill Street Blues, the groundbreaking Steven Bochco hit that aired on the same night as Cosby (it ran 1981 to 1987 and had 98 Emmy nominations). Hill Street went on many "best" lists at the time but young adults today know nothing about it and the cop series is rarely mentioned anymore on the greatest lists.

Instead, today's critics list The Sopranos as one of the best in history. It ended in 2007, yet 25 years from now young adults may be just as clueless about the HBO mob series as people are about Hill Street Blues today.

It has even been stated that television is better now than ever, that we are in the "golden age" of TV. If you go back and look you'll find similar comments made about the medium in the 1950s, early 1970s, mid 1980s and mid 1990s. Every time a few new series attract media attention the idea is again brought up that it's the "best ever."

Don't let yourself be fooled—the current "best ever" claims made regarding shows like Mad Men, Game of Thrones, 30 Rock and Modern Family are virtually meaningless. These programs will all eventually be forgotten by future viewers and replaced by other series that are called the "greatest."

This chapter is an attempt to rectify the bias toward modern series on greatest lists by going back in time to pull together the trend-setting shows from the past, the ones that had the biggest impact on the medium. Many of these haven't been seen in years, while a few are still on the air.

There are a variety of ways to judge which television series were the "greatest":

- One criterion could be how long the show stayed on network television. The longest-running prime time series of all time were on the air for at least 20 years, including 60 Minutes (since 1968), Monday Night Football (since 1970), 20/20 (since 1978), Wonderful World of Disney (for 34 years), The Ed Sullivan Show (24 years), America's Most Wanted (started in 1988), Cops (since 1989), The Simpsons and America's Funniest Home Videos since 1990, and 20 years each for Red Skelton, Gunsmoke, and Law & Order.

    There are programs in other dayparts that have had even longer runs. The Today Show has been on the air since

1952 and The Tonight Show since 1954, while Meet the Press gets the prize for longest-running show still on the air by starting in 1947.

The network evening news programs on CBS and NBC have aired every weekday for over five decades. SportsCenter has aired non-stop since 1979. Saturday Night Live has been on for 37 years. Larry King Live and Oprah were on for 25 years. Wheel of Fortune started on NBC in 1975 and has been in syndication since 1983. And Sesame Street has aired since 1969.

Based on longevity alone these programs deserve some credit as television success stories. But Cops, Larry King, Funniest Home Videos and Wheel of Fortune don't usually make anyone's list of the greatest shows of all time.

- Another measure of worthiness of being named one of the greatest would be the length of time it has aired in reruns. Black and white 1950s shows I Love Lucy and Leave It to Beaver continue to get good ratings on cable. Other programs that kept going in repeats for more than 40 years have included The Andy Griffith Show, Perry Mason, I Dream of Jeannie, The Brady Bunch, Bewitched and Star Trek.

With the new "dot two" HD channels a number of rerun channels have popped up, such as Me-TV and Retro Television. These networks are filled with reruns ranging from former big hits like All in the Family to obscure programs that no one has heard of like The Mothers-in-Law. The 39 episodes of The Honeymooners from 1955 have been in syndication for 55 years and continue to get repeated over and over again in scratchy black and white.

- The number of Emmy Awards won by a series is another mark of its greatness. Frasier holds the comedy record with 37 Emmys and set another record by winning five times for Best Comedy. Best Drama was won four times each by Hill Street Blues, L.A. Law, West Wing and Mad Men. The Amazing Race has won the Reality Show-Competition Emmy eight times, every year the award was given but one.

General Hospital has been named Best Daytime Drama ten times while Jeopardy has been the Outstanding Game Show twelve times. Other programs that have won a large number of trophies include Sesame Street, the Academy Awards telecasts and 60 Minutes.

The Emmys are a chance for the industry to praise itself and let the public know which programs it thinks viewers should watch. It's no surprise that recently low-rated 30 Rock won Best Comedy three times and cable's Mad Men won Best Drama four times in a row—both are about New York media people. Entertainment critics, network executives and producers all love series that deal with the subject that they know best—New York media—and often those programs up being hailed as the greatest series of all time even though they have a small number of viewers.

- Another measure of a program's greatness would be the number of people that watched it. As mentioned earlier in the book, the highest-rated shows since 1960 (when ratings became scientifically valid) are Gunsmoke, The Beverly Hillbillies, Bonanza, Wagon Train, All in the Family, Dallas, and Cosby Show.

Critics will never accept viewership numbers as a measure of greatness because they believe television panders to the lowest common denominator. A show's ratings success may actually work against it appearing on a greatest list. There's no better example than Beverly Hillbillies, the most-watched comedy of all time (over one-third of the country watched) but one that is derided by contemporary media writers that want to make you believe a show like Modern Family (attracting 4% of Americans) is what everyone is watching.

- One more criterion that could be used is how much money a program makes. Ultimately that is what truly decides whether a program is a success since television is primarily a business. But that aspect is also the most difficult to quantify.

It's not as simple as judging a television show by the amount of money a network gets from advertising. The production costs of the program must be taken into account, along with the long-term residual payments to cast members for reruns and how much money the series can get in syndication or on DVD. There are also spin-offs, movie versions and remakes that could increase a show's long-term value.

American Idol and Sunday Night Football far-and-away take in the most money for prime time ads but they certainly don't make the most profit. Idol has high star salaries (Jennifer Lopez reportedly made $20 million a year), huge production costs and doesn't make money from reruns. The Sunday NFL games actually lose money with NBC going hundreds of millions of dollars in the red.

Friends and ER made NBC less profit than some lower-rated shows in prime time because cast members demanded large salaries. High profile actors negotiated a share of syndication income in order to stay on the series, reducing the profitability of reruns. But even with all those expenses, former NBC president Warren Littlefield reports in his book that due to rerun income Friends has generated over $5 billion in revenue, Seinfeld has taken in $4 billion and ER $3 billion. (Seinfeld was so valuable to NBC that the network offered Jerry Seinfeld $5 million a week to continue doing the show but he turned it down.)

Who Wants to Be a Millionaire made $700 million for ABC when it aired in 2000, but it has made little in reruns on GSN. It still does well in syndication, but Disney lost a 2010 lawsuit that awarded $269 million in past licensing fees to the production company.

60 Minutes makes CBS a profit but it has one of the lowest advertising rates in prime time because it attracts one of the oldest audiences on broadcast TV. 60 Minutes charges about one-fifth the amount FOX makes for each American Idol ad even although both are usually top ten shows.

The ideal money-making program is one that doesn't have high production costs, doesn't have to pay a lot to talent, can attract the right demographics, does well in reruns, sells DVDs and makes money through merchandising. Animated series like Spongebob Squarepants and Family Guy match most of those and could be among the biggest profit-makers in TV history.

Note that using the above criteria, only a few series appear to have more than two of them. 60 Minutes is longest-running, has won dozens of Emmy Awards, and was number one in the ratings four times in three different decades (seasons starting in 1979, 1982, 1991 and 1993). Although it has aired some past segments on cable networks but doesn't rerun well, has low ad rates and attracts an older demographic.

Gunsmoke holds the record for the longest-airing non-animated scripted television program with the same lead cast members, and was one of the highest-rated of all time. It also continues to be shown in reruns on TVLand and other cable networks. But it won few awards and attracts an older audience.

All in the Family won Emmy Awards, was the top show on television for five years straight and charged top dollar for ads, but though it continues to air it has not rerun well and looks dated. So it's not easy to pick the "greatest" because no show easily meets all criteria.

What critics consider the top television programs of all time has changed over the years. As new programs come on the air and older series fade into reruns, what people consider "greatest" changes.

As recently as 1998, here is what *Entertainment Weekly* said was the top ten:

1. The Mary Tyler Moore Show
2. Seinfeld
3. All in the Family
4. Cheers
5. The X Files
6. I Love Lucy
7. The Larry Sanders Show
8. Hill Street Blues
9. The Tonight Show
10. The Simpsons

This list reflects the typically myopic view of television history by this entertainment publication. Note that they tend to select comedies and series that were recent (for 1998). The X Files—one of the 10 greatest of all time? The Larry Sanders Show? They were critical favorites but too often programs that are considered "hip" at the time fade quickly into oblivion.

In 2002, *TV Guide* put together its own list:

1. Seinfeld
2. I Love Lucy
3. Honeymooners
4. All in the Family
5. The Sopranos
6. 60 Minutes
7. Late Show with David Letterman
8. The Simpsons
9. The Andy Griffith Show
10. Saturday Night Live

Note that Mary Tyler Moore was missing, Seinfeld was called the greatest as it ended its run, and The Sopranos made the top ten even though it had only been on the air for three years. It's also interesting that Letterman made the *TV Guide* list, but The Tonight Show was picked by *Entertainment Weekly*.

In 2008, the *New York News* tried its hand at a list for television's 60th anniversary of regular prime time programming and it was very eclectic:

1. The Sopranos
2. All in the Family
3. Oprah Winfrey Show
4. American Idol
5. West Wing
6. The Mary Tyler Moore Show
7. Dallas
8. 24
9. Twin Peaks
10. Sesame Street

This group of New York writers selected two New York series for the top of the list and crowned The Sopranos as the top show just a year after it went off the air. They even slipped in urban New York children's show Sesame Street. But 24, Dallas, Twin Peaks and West Wing make this drama-heavy list very unusual.

Entertainment Weekly then put out a 2008 list that named the top 100 TV shows of the past 25 years (since 1983). They intentionally excluded older series that so often make the lists:

1. The Simpsons
2. The Sopranos
3. Seinfeld
4. The X-Files
5. Sex and the City
6. Survivor
7. The Cosby Show
8. Lost
9. Friends
10. Buffy the Vampire Slayer

You have to go online to catch the entire hilariously off-base ranking that places South Park at #12. By dumping any shows from before the Cosby era, it's the ultimate example of that magazine's lack of historical perspective.

In 2012 ABC "News" did a prime time special on the greatest TV shows of all time (though that doesn't seem to be very newsworthy!). Barbara Walters hosted and online voters picked I Love Lucy as the best. Finalists were selected for each genre by TV insiders, then fans picked the winner in each category. Nominees favored modern programs, as usual. For example in the best drama category four of the five had been on the air in the last six years!

If you are searching for Websites with lists, you'll find a bias towards science fiction and drama series. The site TV Vote did a seven-year online survey (2001-2008) of the greatest series of all time and fans placed over ten million votes for 1,733 shows! The winners included Firefly, Xena: Warrior Princess, Bonanza, Gunsmoke, Battlestar Galactica, Buffy, Farscape, Jericho, Angel and Combat!

There are others that have narrowed the lists to the top 50 dramas or greatest game shows. You can even find the "worst TV shows" list, including the 2002 *TV Guide* ranking that placed Jerry Springer as the worst of all time, followed by My Mother the Car, the XFL football league that lasted for three months in 2001, The Brady Bunch Variety Hour, and Hogan's Heroes (even though it was nominated for a Best Comedy Emmy).

One of the most interesting lists came from Steven Stark in his book *Glued to the Set*, where he picked the 60 shows that "made us who we are." His list would be the closest to the selections I make below but Stark added a couple of twists by giving more credence to 1960s shows like Beverly Hillbillies, Mr. Ed, The Smothers Brothers Comedy Hour and The Dating Game. He makes some great points about the impact of these innocuous series on the history of the medium.

What follows is my attempt to give a general overview of what makes the top in each genre. They are not listed in any type of numeric ranking or special order and are not the "best" in terms of quality or audience acceptance. Instead these are the series that had the biggest impact on the medium from a programming perspective.

Game shows are left off the list because few in the industry ever put them on the greatest lists. Reality programming is too new to say which have the most long-term impact, although there is no doubt Amazing Race, Survivor and American Idol have been good shows. Since they are not rerun successfully, chances are that viewers years from now will be as clueless about them as we are today about Arthur Godfrey's Talent Scouts, a top ten singing competition from the 1950s that discovered some top 40 stars.

What you'll find is that many of the greatest TV programs are located in New York or Los Angeles, feature strong male leads, aired on CBS or NBC, and often are related to the entertainment industry. The current hot programs that best reflect that trend are 30 Rock, American Idol, Mad Men and Dancing with the Stars.

CHILDRENS PROGRAMS

Television's impact on children didn't really start with the semi-educational entertainment programs of the late 1940s and early 1950s, such as Howdy Doody, Ding Dong School or Kookla, Fran and Ollie. Instead the show that really changed the way children watch TV was originally called DISNEYLAND and later was known as THE WONDERFUL WORLD OF DISNEY.

The weekly Sunday night series was nothing but an hour-long commercial for Walt Disney. He figured out that children's programming could be used for more than just education—studios could actually make money off related ventures that were promoted on the air.

The well-known movie producer worked a deal with ABC that allowed him to promote his new theme park and movies in a packaged entertainment show that started in 1955.

It was an "anthology" format, hosted by Disney himself, which allowed something different to air each week. Cartoons one Sunday night, Davy Crockett the next, followed by a nature documentary or the young Osmond boys singing at the Disneyland park.

When an episode became popular, Disney sold items to capitalize on it (such as storybooks or coonskin caps) and found ways to duplicate its success (such as reissuing the reedited Crockett TV episodes as a movie in theatres).

After Walt died in 1966, the program remained on the air and opened each week with an animated Tinker Bell flying in front of the landmark Disney castle. In the 1990s, Disney chairman Michael Eisner became the show's awkward host on ABC before the series moved for a short time to the Disney Channel. While the program left the air in 2008, it inspired an industry of children's programming producers to see the tube as not just an educational device but also a marketing tool to young people.

SESEAME STREET premiered in 1969 as a way to fight the commercialization of children's programming. It was created as a non-commercial kid's version of the most popular show on the air at the time in an attempt to teach inner-city children numbers and letters. Like adult hit Laugh-In, the sketches were short, the cast was large, and there were even "commercials" (the show was "brought to you by" letters and numbers).

Most praise the long-running series for what it teaches, but others have pointed out the negative impact of the series. The program has been shown to increase short attention spans in children, forcing educators to use entertainment methods in the classroom. Ironically, when the anniversary DVD set of the original episodes was released in 2009, there had to be a warning label attached since there were so many scenes from forty years earlier that are now considered politically incorrect and bad for kids.

Sesame Street started as an alternative to product-pushing commercial children's programming but is now a moneymaking machine. There are Sesame Street toys, DVDs, CDs, arena shows, clothing, and the always-popular annual Elmo doll for Christmas. Despite winning more Emmy Awards than any other children's show in history, there should be concern about educational children's programming on public television that is now packaged no differently than a commercial series.

Other great family programs for children are from the distant past, including LITTLE HOUSE ON THE PRAIRIE, MR. ROGERS, LEAVE IT TO BEAVER (the first sitcom to revolve around the children instead of the parents), THE MUPPET SHOW and the short musical Saturday morning clips between cartoons called SCHOOLHOUSE ROCK. Despite the fact that there are hundreds of kids' shows on television today, with entire networks devoted to children's programming, there isn't much currently on the air that would be considered classic unless it's more adult-oriented, such as Spongebob Squarepants.

VARIETY PROGRAMS

This was a top format in the original days of television, where a host or set of hosts would introduce a mixture of singers and comedians doing their material in front of a live studio audience.

Few programs were able to bring the quality of entertainment into the living room the way THE ED SULLIVAN SHOW did in the 1950s and 1960s. Known today for its classic performances by every major musical performer from the Beatles to the Rolling Stones to the Jackson 5, it was a true variety series that featured comedians, circus acts, classical artists and pop music. Elvis made his most famous appearance on the show—which later was fictionalized into the musical comedy Bye Bye Birdie (including Sullivan appearing as himself in the film version).

Newspaper columnist Sullivan had no apparent talent and just introduced the guests, much like conductor Lawrence Welk would do on his music program. They both knew how to step out of the way and let the performers shine. That's why Sullivan lasted from 1948 to 1971 and Welk reruns still air Saturday nights on public television.

Unfortunately many young adults today have never heard of these shows that had such a major impact on popularizing music. Two of my college students, one who is pre-med, said they have never even heard of Elvis Presley! How is that possible?

There were other great variety series, like THE CAROL BURNETT SHOW and SONNY & CHER. But none have had the impact of NBC's original SATURDAY NIGHT LIVE. It has launched dozens of major careers and pushed television to become edgier by airing material late at night that prime time shows couldn't get away with. It's main influence is that it made it okay to mock contemporary issues and politics, which was copied by MTV, The Simpsons, The Daily Show, The Colbert Report, Conan O'Brien and even Sesame Street.

NEWS AND TALK PROGRAMS

The longevity of two of the original talk programs is a tribute to the brilliant conception and production of the shows. Pat Weaver, dad of Alien movie star Sigourney Weaver, created the two shows that would start and end the day on NBC. They have been copied dozens of times but rarely equaled.

THE TODAY SHOW was innovative in a number of firsts—it had the first woman co-host of a news show, the first black co-host of a news show, the first use of satellites and first mixture of news and entertainment. The fact that it has been going strong since 1952 means it has had a major impact, to the point that most early morning competitors have attempted to copy it. Today's expansion to a third and fourth hour may have diluted the program's impact (with the final hour devoted to daily live on the air drinking with Hoda and Kathie Lee). It still usually tops the morning show ratings but Good Morning America beat it a few weeks in 2012.

THE TONIGHT SHOW premiered in 1954 on the NBC network, creating another concept that has been copied by many others. The opening monolog, band leader, humorous side kick, sketches, audience questions, man-on-the-street interviews, standup comics, late-in-the-show musical guests, stars sitting on a couch next to the host—all were first put together on this program. Steve Allen started it as a variety show, Jack Paar added the host chat element, then Johnny Carson perfected it and turned it into an institution by hosting The Tonight Show for almost 30 years. The 2010 hosting struggle between Conan O'Brien and Jay Leno proves the importance of the program's profits to NBC.

60 MINUTES is currently the longest-running prime time series but it took a few years after it started in 1968 for it to became the first popular "news magazine." In its early days it was low-rated and only on every other week. It did so poorly that CBS moved it to Sunday afternoons.

Soon it became known for hard-hitting exposés by in-your-face reporters and the ratings climbed. The show's creator, the late Don Hewitt, produced the series for almost 40 years and favored filmed pieces that were historical perspectives. Although today it has one of the oldest audiences on TV, in recent years a new producer has take over and implemented more contemporary segments of newsworthy events. It ended the 2012 season ranked 16th in the ratings, amazing for a 45-year-old series.

LATE NITE WITH DAVID LETTERMAN was the hip 1980s NBC show that was the first to make late night talk popular with young people. Where Carson attracted the middle-aged sleepyheads, Letterman's wacky humor appealed to younger adults who stayed up later to watch gimmicks like stupid pet tricks. His concept originated as an Emmy-winning NBC 9 a.m. morning show (which lasted for four months in 1980) before it moved to late evening. He has been less successful repeating the format at CBS since 1993, where he usually gets lower ratings than Jay Leno's Tonight Show but had a brief surge in 2009-2010 when he was up against Conan and after his affair with a female employee was exposed.

THE OPRAH WINFREY SHOW made the host the queen of television daytime. Starting as a topical series in 1986 with the star roaming the audience, in later years Oprah's program evolved into spiritual Winfrey ruling from her throne on the stage, reading questions off the TelePrompTer. At some point Oprah became more interesting to watch than her guests (about the time she wheeled out that wagon with fat on it), and the series ended up revolving around Winfrey reacting to the subject matter. When students in my talk show class would conduct serious research of her program they found that she was lightweight, biased, self-centered and not as profound as fans claimed. But no one can argue with her success at inspiring millions to market themselves just as well as she does.

This list could also include some of the past evening newscasts, such as THE CBS EVENING NEWS WITH WALTER CRONKITE. But the modern program with some of the greatest influence is THE DAILY SHOW. It started as a less-political comedy series with former ESPN anchor Craig Kilbourn. When Jon Stewart took over in 1999, the show took on a much more liberal political bent while retaining the mockery of news programming. It has been a ratings hit, a big Emmy winner (winning Best Variety Show nine years in a row!) and has impacted the political process by influencing the way its young adult audience votes.

DRAMATIC PROGRAMS

Long before Law & Order or Boston Legal, PERRY MASON was the first one-hour drama to show a lawyer trying to solve crimes (up until then police solved crimes in a half-hour format). While defending his client he managed to call witnesses that squirmed while Mason dramatically revealed the killer at the end of each episode (he only lost one case).

The fact that this 1957-1966 black-and-white series is the only '50s non-western drama that is still aired in local syndication proves that people enjoy the way it told a story. The original cast was reunited for a series of highly-rated TV movies in the late 1980s and early 1990s. It even has had an influence on the legal system—2009 Supreme Court Justice appointee Sonia Sotomayor told her Senate confirmation committee that it was watching Perry Mason reruns that gave her a love of the law. And when she admitted it, Minnesota Senator (and former TV comedian) Al Franken said it was the series his family watched together as well.

STAR TREK was conceived as a "space western," though today the original at times looks like a spaced-out soap opera. Just about every science fiction show since has had to live up to Star Trek, including the program's own four spin-offs and multiple film versions. That's pretty good for a series that never ranked in the top 30 and was cancelled twice. Not only does the 1966-69 program still do well in reruns, but it continues to sell merchandise and appearances by even minor actors at a convention can attract thousands of visitors.

THE TWILIGHT ZONE was a science fiction anthology that first went on in 1959, but sponsors didn't care for the show because it was difficult to figure out. The scripts were smart—almost to the point that people couldn't understand them. Host Rod Serling tried to make a social statement through absurd plots involving what seemed to be a parallel earth. And writers since have tried to copy it, including Lost creator J. J. Abrams, who called Twilight Zone "perhaps the best show ever on television." It even inspired the Tower of Terror ride at Walt Disney World. The series has been revived three times—once on CBS in 1985, then in syndication in 1987, and again on UPN in 2002.

HILL STREET BLUES was the first modern gritty cop show, created by Steven Bochco in 1981. Unlike other weekly dramas that solved crime in an hour, this one didn't neatly tie up the plot at the end of each episode. Sometimes it ended with a cop being killed or a murderer being set free by the system. It also introduced to network prime time some of the same street language that later peppered Bochco's NYPD Blue.

GUNSMOKE is the longest-running scripted drama that used the same cast (Law and Order tied its 20 years in 2010 but has used different casts). This classic western started as a half-hour television adoption of a popular radio series (the show ran simultaneously on radio and TV for six years). The televised version had 635 episodes from 1955 to 1975 and was the number one show for four years straight. The program's success led to other top-rated westerns like Wagon Train and Bonanza, although Gunsmoke's impact has declined a bit with the death of the western as a viable program format on modern TV.

There are other modern series that some will argue should be included as the greatest, such as The Sopranos, CSI, Lost and ER (winner of the 2012 ABC News online voting for best drama of all time). But it's difficult to know whether those contemporary dramas will do well in reruns or if they have long-term influence on the medium. When Lost ended in 2010, *USA Today* actually called it "one of TV's greatest series—at any time, of any genre, on any platform." The paper then mirrored others in the press by saying that "Lost will stay with us for a long, long time." But there is no way of knowing that and already the show is rarely talked about. The fact is that viewers rarely watch reruns of decades-old dramas.

SITCOMS

Unlike dramas, sitcoms do very well in reruns and can last for decades in syndicated repeats. That's why there are more comedies on most "greatest" lists than any other television genre.

I LOVE LUCY was on the top of the list in my book *TV's Greatest Sitcoms* because it revolutionized the medium. Lucy and her husband Desi owned their own production studio (a first for a woman) and hired someone to create the process that allowed the filming of a three-camera live studio audience program in California (at that time the only way to do TV was either live with three-cameras on the east coast or a single-camera filmed series). Lucy led a small screen revolution, which saw most productions move to Hollywood. The fact that the 1951 series is still airing today in reruns proves that audiences really do love Lucy.

THE DICK VAN DYKE SHOW is one of the rare 1960s shows that is considered classic. It was a classy contemporary workplace comedy that was a contrast to that era's fantasy family sitcoms like Bewitched, I Dream of Jeannie and Beverly Hillbillies. The Van Dyke Show was firmly planted in the reality of the life of Carl Reiner, who based the series on his own career as a writer for a hit live TV variety show in the early 1950s. The lead characters (Van Dyke and Mary Tyler Moore) were patterned after John and Jackie Kennedy, and in 2008 Michelle Obama listed this show as her favorite series of all time.

ALL IN THE FAMILY was probably the single most pivotal program in TV history. Nothing before it was as "in your face," topical or combative, while every comedy after it tried to copy the show's success. The 1971 series about the four fighting family members (bigoted dad Archie, scatter-brained wife Edith, ditzy daughter Gloria and her liberal live-in husband Michael) used language that had never been heard on television before to discuss topics that were rarely mentioned on the tube. It perfectly reflected society's struggle between conservatives and liberals during the Vietnam War era. After a low-rated start, it was the number one show on TV from 1972 to 1977. It also led to five spin-offs, including The Jeffersons and Maude.

M*A*S*H was called by *Entertainment Weekly* "TV's most socially redeeming sitcom." It was supposed to be about radical doctors in the operating room during the Korean War, but writers not so subtly included 1970s issues in the scripts. It was made by anti-war people who used Korea as the platform to try to convince viewers that the Vietnam War was futile. After 11 years, the show ended with the highest-rated episode in TV history.

THE MARY TYLER MOORE SHOW was an innovative 1970 series about a 30-year-old single woman trying to make it in the male business of television. Not as edgy or as highly rated as All in the Family, Mary Tyler Moore Show was considered the greatest TV series in history for almost two decades. *Entertainment Weekly* called it the #1 show of all time; *TV Guide* picked its humorous take on a clown's funeral as the #1 single episode of all time; the show's hat-tossing opening was ranked as the #2 TV event of all time (next to the Kennedy assassination) in *TV Guide*; and until 2002 it had the most Emmys awards of any prime time scripted comedy (Frasier surpassed it).

The Mary Tyler Moore Show worked because it had the right balance of what was going on in the world at the time—innocence and skepticism. It is often copied (Murphy Brown and 30 Rock replicate the oddball characters on a TV staff). And its influence reached out to dozens of famous women, from Oprah to Diane Sawyer, who say Mary inspired them to go into television.

THE COSBY SHOW resurrected the family comedy genre that had been pronounced dead on TV in 1984. Cosby's first year was so well done that it was immediately named Best Comedy at the Emmys. And the next five years it ranked number one in the Nielsens. Today the Cosby Show appears merely cute with many of the episodes padded with music at the end to fill a half hour. It caused an increase in minority-family sitcoms, but books have now been written claiming The Cosby Show may have actually done more harm than good to the minority community by setting unrealistic expectations.

SEINFELD was the last big hit comedy on the tube, the perfect reflection of the daycare mentality of the '90s where four unrelated people were stuck in a room together—talking, eating, fighting, laughing, lying, calling each other names, and coming back together as friends the next day. It was a flop in its first couple of seasons until it moved to Thursday night, and even then it only twice was the number one show on television. It's success caused sitcoms to move away from their family base, which also led to the near demise of the situation comedy genre by the mid-2000s.

THE SIMPSONS needs to be included just because of longevity and the amount of merchandising money it has brought FOX. The characters started as a segment on the Tracy Ullman variety show, then they had a TV special in 1989 before its regular series run began in 1990. It is the longest-running scripted series in history and led to prime time's acceptance of other animated shows like Family Guy and South Park. But, as noted previously, it has a long history of mediocre ratings that would have cancelled any other series years ago.

THE GREATEST PRIME TIME LINEUP IN TV HISTORY

In the fall of 1973, CBS had a Saturday Night lineup that is still considered the greatest of all time.

Saturday used to be a night when people stayed home to watch great television. The 1973 program log included All in the

Family, M*A*S*H, The Mary Tyler Moore Show, The Bob Newhart Show, and The Carol Burnett Show. Those programs were scheduled together for only one year before some were moved to other nights, but it was an amazing block that allowed for complete audience flow for three hours straight.

The only thing that has come close since has been the 1994 "Must See TV" NBC Thursday night lineup of Mad About You, Friends, Seinfeld, and ER. The only problem was an 8:30 show called "Madman of the People" with Dabney Coleman that ranked 12th but was cancelled after it lost 25% of the audience in between Seinfeld and ER.

NBC head programmer Warren Littlefield wrote in his 2012 book *Top of the Rock* that he actually thinks NBC's 1984 Thursday lineup was better, calling it the "Night of Bests." It had Cosby Show, Family Ties, Cheers, Night Court and Hill Street Blues. Okay, those are good—but Night Court is the weak spot. Despite NBC's hype of Thursday night, it just never could pull together a complete three-hour hit schedule. And in retrospect you don't see a lot of people now watching Mad About You or Family Ties reruns either.

Others have tried to schedule a great block of programs, such as CBS on Monday night in 1991 (Murphy Brown, Designing Women and Northern Exposure), ABC's TGIF lineup in 1989, and FOX's current Sunday night animated block. It proves that it is difficult for a network to get people to stay tuned in through an entire night's programming. That is why the Saturday night CBS lineup from 1973, a night of all hits, lives on as the greatest of all.

HOW HIT SHOWS DO IN RERUNS

There are programs that earned big ratings or won coveted awards when they were first on the air that have faded with time. Those series had little long-term impact, and looking back people have to wonder what viewers or Emmy voters were thinking.

This group would include '60s sitcoms like BEWITCHED, which was once the number two show on television, HOGAN'S HEROES (a comedy about a Nazi concentration camp) and the top-rated BEVERLY HILLBILLIES. All three series, which few watch in reruns today because they seem so corny, were even nominated for the Best Comedy Emmy award.

Then there was the '80s fad of the prime time soap operas, such as DYNASTY, FALCON CREST and DALLAS, which was the highest-rated drama in TV history. Now they seem dated and are almost unwatchable in reruns, even though they occasionally pop up on cable networks. (Cable network TNT revived Dallas in 2012 with much of the original cast.)

There were also the '80s female empowerment comedies, many which continue to air on cable. MURPHY BROWN, DESIGNING WOMEN, and ROSEANNE were all huge hits and winners of multiple Emmys. Some rerun better than others, but the stilted anti-male bias seems dated. GOLDEN GIRLS, which was from the same era and was the first TV show with an all-female cast of regulars, has aged better than the rest.

HBO series also fall into this category because the "cutting edge" programs with profanity, violence and nudity are somewhat popular when they first air but are often forgotten years later. For every hit like SOPRANOS and SEX AND THE CITY, there are a dozen HBO series that don't rerun well such as OZ, DEADWOOD, and SIX FEET UNDER. Many were hot at the time but are rarely heard from again, such as THE LARRY SANDERS SHOW, 1ST AND TEN and ARLISS. More recent series like CURB YOUR ENTHUSIASM and ENTOURAGE are recut for syndication but may well be forgotten twenty years from now.

There is no better example of the lack of long-term impact from HBO than a 1990 show called DREAM ON. The series, about a New York book editor who thinks about old movies while making love to women, won Emmy nominations (rare for HBO back then) and was picked as a critical favorite (another New York media show!). It lasted on the air for six years and was produced by the team that went on the create Friends—yet today no one even recalls it, much less watches it.

Many HBO series are timepieces for the period in which they are made. The impact of HBO shows are probably more pronounced when they first air because people pay to see them, can watch them multiple times each week and are R-rated escapism you can't see on normal television. But that impression fades with time as they are replaced by newer, edgier series.

If you want to object and claim that HBO programs are among the greatest, then the question is—will you be watching those HBO shows in reruns 20 years from now? If you think the answer is yes, then just remind yourself of Dream On.

Compare those cutting-edge programs to less successful network series that only later became popular in syndicated reruns. You just never know what program will be hot years later or what flop series will become successful in reruns or on DVD.

LEAVE IT TO BEAVER didn't even make the top 25 of the ratings when it ran from 1957 to 1963, yet The Cleavers continues to be referenced today as the ideal family and it remains one of the top shows rerun on TVLand.

The BRADY BUNCH also was not a hit when it aired in prime time from 1969-1974. Only later did it become the most resurrected show in history (Brady Bunch Variety Hour, The Brady Brides, a Brady Bunch cartoon, The Bradys drama, and the My Fair Brady reality series). Its stars still are regular ratings-grabbers when they guest star on current shows, so expect to see these grown-up Brady kids on television for decades to come.

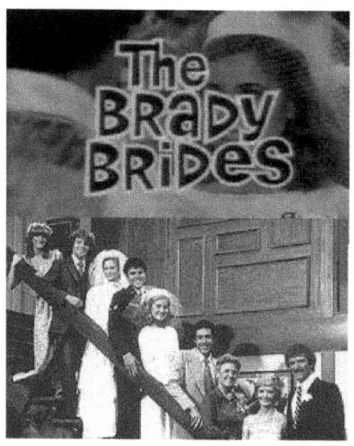

IS SEINFELD THE GREATEST?

Seinfeld, the sitcom most recently proclaimed by *TV Guide* as the greatest show of all time, started on TV over 20 years ago and has now been off network television for 15 years. Today's young adults can't even recall seeing the original episodes when they first aired on network prime time.

When the final NBC episode aired on May 14, 1998, it was only the third time in history that the highest-rated series on TV stopped making new episodes, following I Love Lucy and The Andy Griffith Show. Those earlier series kept characters alive through spin-offs (The Lucy/Desi Comedy Hour and Mayberry R.F.D.), while Seinfeld said he would never do a reunion (which was spoofed when Curb Your Enthusiasm brought the actors back to portray themselves as part of a fake reunion show).

I decided to watch all 180 syndicated half hours to try to determine how Seinfeld measures up to others that are now considered classics. My conclusion, as stated in an article that I wrote for *TV Quarterly*, is that Seinfeld was clever and often humorous but not consistently the greatest. It certainly is a very good way to pass a half hour and some individual episodes are classics, but overall it may not quite match the hype it is accorded.

The early episodes of the show are weak, in part due to the fact that the first 16 aired over a period of two years. The pilot (with a very toned-down Kramer character, no musical transitions between long scenes and no Elaine) is under-whelming, unlike the instant-classic pilots of All in the Family, The Mary Tyler Moore Show and The Cosby Show.

After the Seinfeld pilot was shown in 1989 and four episodes aired in the summer of 1990, the show returned for its third try in January of 1991. The low-rated series then left the air for another couple months and returned in April of 1991. By fall of 1991 the series settled into its Wednesday night slot and the episodes gained momentum.

Episode 22 featured a tough-talking library cop who pursued Jerry's 20-year overdo book, followed the next week by a half hour set entirely in a mall parking garage. By early 1992 classic episodes appeared with regularity, including "The Pez Dispenser," "The Boyfriend" and "The Fix-Up" (about a defective condom, which won the Emmy for Outstanding Comedy Writing).

The fourth season produced consistent winners, with plots ranging from Jerry and George selling a TV pilot to the irreverent treatment of a bubble boy. It was also the year of "The Virgin," "The Junior Mint," and "The Contest," as well as an episode dealing with Jerry picking his nose in public.

It was during this creative peak that the series was permanently moved to Thursday nights. Seinfeld experienced a dramatic increase in viewership for many classic episodes, such as "The Puffy Shirt" and "The Soup Nazi," which is so incredibly well written and performed that it just gets better with age.

After co-creator Larry David left the series, the eighth and ninth seasons contained a few fun bits (Elaine's dance moves or George getting smarter due to abstinence) but too many episodes didn't measure up to previous seasons. Characters at times became caricatures, such as in "The Dealership" where they all scream and flail their arms while Jerry tries to buy a car (it was the first original episode to air after NBC announced the show was going to end and was a poorly-timed disappointment).

The final season sputtered to the much-maligned finale. The series ended with an inconsistency that hadn't occurred with previous sitcoms that are considered classics, such as the highly-rated M*A*S*H finale or The Mary Tyler Moore Show's group hug. Seinfeld's attempt to bring together guest stars from past seasons for the final episode was a noble try but putting the regulars on trial for not helping a petty crime victim was a thin premise and the final scene in the jail cell is a disappointing ending.

Watching the show in daily syndication today just magnifies the unevenness that may not have been as noticeable when the original episodes aired once a week. The program was filled with rage, bigotry and misogyny. Violence, Nazism and death were used as punch lines and made lead characters look unsympathetic. The final episode that Larry David wrote before leaving the series was "The Invitations," a callused satire that had George's fiancé dropping dead after licking old wedding invitation envelopes while he walked away happy to be rid of her.

The soulless Seinfeld characters went beyond just being amoral to often being immoral without suffering any consequences (until the over-the-top finale, which put them in jail but seemed to mock the idea of restitution). Watching Jerry steal a loaf of bread from a little old lady ("The Rye") may be slapstick funny in a writers' meeting but without some type of moral resolution at the end of the episode he came across more like Homer Simpson than a legitimate human being.

Which leads to the biggest conclusion that I came to after watching the entire series: Seinfeld was the human version of a cartoon. It was not meant to be real and almost begged the audience to not believe what the leads were getting away with. Jerry not only made frequent references to his desire to be a cartoon superhero, but his Superman doll was prominently displayed on his living room shelf. One of the last episodes in the final season was even titled "The Cartoon," where Jerry revealed he had drawings of Lois Lane naked.

References to Clark Kent included 1994's "The Race," where Jerry's girlfriend is named Lois, the theme song from the Superman movie is played when Jerry competes against an old schoolmate and Seinfeld ends the show quoting Superman as he turns to wink at the camera. The show's star was telling viewers that this whole thing was a fantasy, like the cartoon genre he loves so much.

Jerry even used the comparison to the show's cartoonish plotlines in interviews. When the cast reunited in 2009 for Curb Your Enthusiasm, Seinfeld said his favorite episode of the original show was "The Pothole," saying "That really was a Road Runner moment, when you get to have one of your characters (Newman) totally engulfed in flames, and the next week they're back as good as new."

Seinfeld was written to be unrealistic, with fake holidays, politically incorrect jokes and absurd contests. When George talked you could almost see the little bubble above the head of a depressed Charlie Brown. Kramer was like Wile E. Coyote, getting knocked down and bouncing back up with no long-term effect. It should be no surprise then that Jerry's first follow-up project after the sitcom stopped was an animated movie about bees.

Seinfeld certainly does not deserve the title "the greatest TV show of all time," but its cartoonish style makes it easy to watch in syndication. Its reruns will stay popular as long as the family situation comedy is dead on network TV.

Chapter Seven Discussion Questions

1. How have the shows that are considered "greatest" changed over the years?
2. What are the criteria that can be used in deciding what shows are the greatest?
3. What shows make most of the top ten lists printed here?
4. What are common characteristics of the greatest shows?
5. What is Disney's long-lasting impact on children's television? What's ironic about Sesame Street today compared to how it started?
6. How can a variety host you have never heard of have an impact on you today?
7. What was the Letterman show's origin and unusual scheduling history?
8. Since dramas are so successful on prime time today, why are few included on the greatest lists?
9. How did Lucy change the TV filming process?
10. What was The Dick Van Dyke Show based on?
11. What series was "the single most pivotal program in TV history"? Why?
12. Why has The Cosby Show's success faded over the years?

13. Explain what is considered the greatest prime time lineup in history.
14. What types of shows were incredibly successful when first on the air but in retrospect are not considered classics?
15. Explain Dream On and what point it teaches you.
16. What did the author do to find out if Seinfeld's show was the greatest of all time? What did he conclude about it?
17. How can the author claim that Seinfeld was a "cartoon"?

REFERENCED BOOKS

Andrejevic, Mark. *Reality TV.* Lanham, MD: Rowman and Littlefield, 2003.

Brooks, Tim and Earle Marsh. *The Complete Directory to Prime Time Network and Cable TV Shows.* New York: Ballantine Books, 2007.

Burnett, Mark. *Jump In!* New York: Ballantine Books, 2006.

Jones, Gerard. *Honey, I'm Home.* New York: St. Martin's, 1993.

Littlefield, Warren. *Top of the Rock.* New York: Doubleday, 2012.

Murray, Susan and Laurie Ouellette. *Reality TV.* New York: NYU Press, 2008.

Postman, Neil. *Amusing Ourselves to Death.* New York: Penguin Books, 2005.

Stallings, Penny. *Forbidden Channels* by Penny Stallings New York: Perennial, 1991.

Stark, Steven. *Glued to the Set.* Concord, CA: Delta Books, 1998.

Winzenburg, Stephen. *TV's Greatest Sitcoms.* Baltimore: PublishAmerica, 2004.

Winzenburg, Stephen. *TV's Greatest Talk Shows.* Baltimore: PublishAmerica, 2005.

INDEX OF SELECTED TOPICS

A la carte cable, 116

Appointment shows, 25-28

Big Ten network, 41-42

Block programming, 33-34, 143

Branding, 44-47

Burnett, Mark, 28, 88

C3, 53

Cable subscriber numbers, 43

Cancellation, 76, 88-89

CATV, 37-39

Censorship in TV history, 96-98

Counterprogramming, 33

ESPN, 40, 44-47, 55, 59, 65-67, 73

Fairmont cable, 22-24, 37

FCC and children's TV, 116

Hammock, 33

Head-to-head programming, 31-33

HBO, 38-39, 54, 80, 85, 95, 144-145

L.O.P theory, 26-27, 33

Must carry, 40

Must See TV, 88, 143

Olympics ratings, 59-60

Pediatricians, 11, 110

Pilots, 29-30

Pitches, 28-31

Ratings of #1 shows, 71-73

Reality TV defined, 124

Retransmission, 40-42

Season length, 84-87

Seinfeld, 24, 62-63, 84, 130, 142, 146-149

Smartest people in TV, 14

Strong lead-in, 33, 88

Super Bowl ratings, 60-61

Spinning ratings, 52, 57-67

Television definition, 19-20

TGIF, 33-34

Who Wants to Be A Millionaire, 33, 41, 87, 129

www.ingramcontent.com/pod-product-compliance
Lightning Source LLC
Chambersburg PA
CBHW070454100426
42743CB00010B/1612